ASVAB STUDY GUIDE

- YOUR BEST EXAM PREP IN JUST 28 DAYS -

ACHIEVE YOUR MILITARY DREAM CAREER ON THE
FIRST TRY WITH 170+ PRACTICE TESTS AND
ADVANCED MEMORIZATION STRATEGIES

ARMED FORCES PREP SPECIALIST

Copyright 2023 by Armed Forces Prep Specialist – All right reserved

DOWNLOAD YOUR FREE BONUS NOW!

We have some exclusive bonus materials for you as a way of saying thank you and to further enhance your experience. These extras include:

- **BONUS 1: Advanced Memorization Strategies**
- **BONUS 2: Anxiety Management - Techniques for Maintaining Calm and Focus**

To claim these valuable resources go to:

https://micolipublishing.wixsite.com/asvab

TABLE OF CONTENT

CHAPTER 1 - INTRODUCTION TO THE ASVAB

COMPREHENSIVE OVERVIEW OF THE ASVAB

Starting the process of learning about the Armed Services Vocational Aptitude Battery (ASVAB) is like getting ready for a big event in your life, especially if you want to enlist in the military. The ASVAB is a thorough evaluation instrument that is more than simply a test and has a significant impact on how prospective military members will develop in the future. The purpose of this guide is to give a comprehensive overview of the ASVAB, setting the groundwork for in-depth study in the upcoming chapters.

Fundamentally, the ASVAB is a multifaceted test intended to assess a broad spectrum of competencies. It's an expression of the various demands and difficulties that one could encounter in a military setting. The exam covers a number of topics, each designed to gauge a particular set of skills. The breadth of knowledge areas covered by the ASVAB, which ranges from mechanical comprehension to general science, ensures a comprehensive evaluation of a candidate's aptitude.

The ASVAB's carefully designed framework includes several subtests that target distinct skill sets. The following subtests are part of the assessment: Mechanical Comprehension, Assembling Objects, Electronics Information, Auto and Shop Information, Word Knowledge, Arithmetic Reasoning, Mathematics Knowledge, and Paragraph Comprehension. In order to provide a complete picture of a candidate's talents, each of these sections looks into various aspects of their intelligence and aptitude.

The ASVAB is more than just an exam to enter the armed forces. It serves as a doorway to recognizing one's areas of strength and growth, providing insights that are beneficial for both personal and military development. The exam promotes a learning attitude that is advantageous in many spheres of life by encouraging a deeper engagement with a variety of disciplines.

ASVAB preparation requires self-control and commitment. It's an opportunity to delve into diverse subjects, challenge oneself, and emerge more knowledgeable and confident. The process of preparation is as rewarding as the test itself, offering a chance to acquire new knowledge, hone existing skills, and develop a well-rounded intellectual profile.

In summary, the ASVAB is a thorough evaluation instrument that provides a window into an individual's abilities and potential, not just a stepping stone to the military. Remember that the main goal of the ASVAB is to provide a valid measure of your preparedness and suitability for a career in the United States Armed Forces. In the next chapters, when we delve deeper into each element of the test, this will become evident. Your journey to a prosperous and satisfying military career begins with this book, which will assist you in navigating the complexities of the ASVAB.

THE IMPORTANCE OF THE ASVAB FOR YOUR MILITARY CAREER

Anyone hoping to work in the US military must pass the Armed Services Vocational Aptitude Battery, or ASVAB. It's more than just an exam; it's a starting point for a rewarding career serving the country. It is impossible to undermark enough how important the ASVAB is to how your military career unfolds. It's a thorough evaluation of your abilities that pinpoints the military occupational specialties (MOS) that best fit your interests and skill set.

It's critical to comprehend the ASVAB's significance to your military career. This exam serves as a tool to assist match your skills to the requirements of the military, so you can pursue a profession where you can succeed and make a meaningful contribution. It's more than just an academic examination.

The 10 subtests that comprise the ASVAB are designed to target several ability sets, such as verbal, mathematical, technical, and spatial abilities. Your success in these domains is crucial since it establishes your suitability for different military positions. The greater your score, the greater the array of career options that become accessible to you.

The Armed Forces Qualification Test (AFQT) score, which is one of the main components of the ASVAB, is determined by taking four subtests: Paragraph Comprehension, Mathematics Knowledge, Word Knowledge, and Arithmetic Reasoning. Your entire eligibility to serve in the military is determined by this number, which makes it very important. You must receive the minimum AFQT score necessary by each branch of the military in order to enroll.

Your results in the other ASVAB areas hold equivalent significance as the AFQT. They assess your fit for particular military positions. Strong points in General Science and Word Knowledge, on the other hand, may place you in a more analytical function. For example, a high score in Mechanical Comprehension or Electronic Information could lead to technical responsibilities.

Let's examine a few examples of how military careers and ASVAB scores correlate. An Army position such as Infantryman, for example, requires a minimum CO (Combat) line score of 87, whereas a position such as Cryptologic Linguist requires high scores in areas such as Skilled Technical (ST). Similar to this, technical positions in the Air Force may call for high line scores in Mechanical (MM) or Electrical (EL).

Recalling that the ASVAB is an ongoing opportunity is crucial. You have the option to retake the exam if your initial results fall short of what is needed for your intended career. You can raise your scores and increase the range of military careers you can pursue thanks to this flexibility. However, since retake exams can be difficult and time-consuming, it's imperative to study well for each attempt.

To sum up, the ASVAB is a crucial stage in your military career. This all-encompassing evaluation assists in matching your abilities to the appropriate military position, guaranteeing a happy and prosperous military career. Keep in mind the importance of the ASVAB and the chances it offers as you study. Your scores can lead to a fulfilling military career if you put in the necessary effort and prepare well.

HOW TO MAKE THE MOST OF THIS GUIDE

Starting the process of getting ready for the ASVAB can be exciting and intimidating at the same time. This guide is meant to accompany you on this trip by providing a thorough method for learning the skills and knowledge required to succeed. It's crucial to comprehend this guide's structure and how each part may be used to improve your learning process if you want to get the most out of it.

The two main portions of the handbook are divided into two areas: theoretical knowledge and practical application. The theoretical part offers comprehensive rationales and insights while exploring the topics included in the ASVAB. This is about more than just scanning the facts; it's about getting a deep comprehension of the ideas that underpin the ASVAB subjects. This section's chapters are devoted to particular ASVAB topics, like word knowledge and arithmetic reasoning, among others. These chapters aim to impart knowledge while also encouraging understanding and critical thinking. Each subject's practical examinations are included in the guide to supplement the theoretical learning. These tests offer a realistic practice experience because they are made to resemble the format and style of the ASVAB simulation test. You can determine where you need further study and how well you comprehend the subject by taking these exams. The iterative nature of these tests is essential to their usefulness. Examine your responses after taking each test, paying particular attention to the wrong ones. You will discover thorough answers and justifications for every question at the conclusion of every chapter. Here is where the true learning takes place: realizing not just the answer that is correct, but also the reasoning behind it.

Two special supplementary chapters on advanced learning strategies and anxiety control are also included in the handbook. The chapter on advanced learning techniques presents methods that can improve memory retention and hasten the learning process. These methods can be used for any learning activity and are not limited to ASVAB preparation. In particular, the chapter on anxiety management is crucial. It tackles exam-day anxiety, one of the most prevalent problems encountered by test-takers. This chapter offers helpful hints and mental drills to help you stay composed and focused so that all of your hard work and preparation pay off on test day.

It is advised to adhere to a planned study plan in order to get the most out of this book. Set aside certain hours to study each subject, and adhere to your timetable. To maximize your study time, apply the advanced learning techniques. Use the practice exams to assess your knowledge on a regular basis and monitor your development. Above all, remember that nervousness is not a reason to underestimate your skills. Utilize the techniques for reducing anxiety to keep your composure and confidence.

Essentially, this manual is an empowerment tool rather than only an informational compilation. It is intended to provide you skills, knowledge, and mental toughness. Remember that every chapter, exam, and tactic in this book is a step closer to your objective of earning a good ASVAB score and a fulfilling military career as you peruse its pages. Your commitment to success and this guide's extensive content combine to make for a powerful combination.

CHAPTER 2 - DETAILED ANALYSIS OF THE ASVAB

STRUCTURE AND FORMATS OF THE EXAM

One essential evaluation instrument that the US military uses is the Armed Services Vocational Aptitude Battery (ASVAB). For prospective service members, it is essential in establishing their eligibility and possible career routes. Comprehending the ASVAB's structure and format is crucial for successful preparation.

Components of the ASVAB

1. **General Science**: This subtest assesses a candidate's understanding of fundamental scientific concepts in great detail. Physics, environmental science, earth science, biology and chemistry are just a few of the many subjects it covers. Questions could cover everything from simpler principles like knowing how cells are put together in biology to more complicated concepts like physics' rules of motion. This portion evaluates a candidate's basic scientific knowledge, which is important for those seeking technical positions in the armed forces.

2. **Arithmetic Reasoning**: This section assesses a person's aptitude for handling common mathematical issues. It comprises simpler tasks using percentages, ratios, elementary algebra, and word problems, as well as more difficult ones including addition, subtraction, multiplication, and division. This section focuses on using mathematical logic to solve problems in practical settings and on problem-solving strategies. These abilities are crucial for jobs requiring precise and fast decision-making.

3. **Word Knowledge**: The scope and depth of a candidate's vocabulary are assessed on this subtest. It has questions that test your knowledge of synonyms, antonyms, and how to properly use words in sentences. This area is not just about having a large vocabulary; it's also about being able to convey complicated ideas clearly and understandably, which is essential in any military capacity.

4. **Paragraph Comprehension**: The comprehension and interpretation of textual content are assessed in this part. In order to answer questions on the primary idea, supporting facts, inferences, and author's goal, applicants must read passages and provide their thoughts. This subtest is crucial for assessing a candidate's ability to process written orders, manuals, and reports, which are common in military operations.

5. **Mathematics Knowledge**: The comprehension of mathematical ideas and their applications is evaluated in this subtest. It consists of probability, statistics, geometry, and algebra questions. This component assesses both the theoretical knowledge of mathematics and the practical application of that knowledge, which is critical for technical and engineering roles in the armed forces.

6. **Electronics Information**: This section tests knowledge of electrical principles and terminologies. It includes questions on circuits, currents, batteries, and electronic devices. This subtest is particularly important for candidates interested in roles related to electronics and electrical engineering.

7. **Auto and Shop Information**: This subtest assesses proficiency in shop procedures, automobile maintenance, and repair. It covers topics including engine parts, car upkeep, and fundamentals of metal and woodworking. This section is designed for applicants who want to work in engineering support, vehicle maintenance, or military logistics.

8. **Mechanical Comprehension**: The comprehension of mechanical and physical principles is evaluated in this part. It contains inquiries on simple machinery, gears, pulleys, and levers. Candidates interested in positions requiring a solid understanding of mechanics, such as those in the military, aviation, or mechanical fields, should take this subtest.

9. **Assembling Objects**: This subtest assesses spatial orientation and the capacity to see the relationships between items. It contains questions that call for candidates to mentally put together things or decipher schematics. For positions requiring spatial awareness and the capacity to comprehend and analyze technical drawings, this portion is crucial.

Formats of the Exam

1. **CAT-ASVAB**: ASVAB's Computerized Adaptive assessment format is a cutting-edge method of standardized assessment. With this style, the test's difficulty adjusts to the test-taker's aptitude. After answering a question properly, the next one gets harder, and after answering a question wrong, the next one gets easy. An evaluation of

a candidate's talents that is more accurate is made possible by this adaptive mechanism. When compared to the paper-and-pencil version, the CAT-ASVAB is renowned for its testing efficiency because it usually takes less questions to effectively assess a candidate's abilities.

2. **Paper-and-Pencil ASVAB**: The paper-and-pencil version of the ASVAB is the standard format. This structure, which is independent of the test-taker's skill level, has a predetermined set of questions. It is frequently given in MEPS, schools, or other military locations. When automated testing is not practical, this form is recommended. While it gives all candidates an equal testing experience, it might take longer to finish than the CAT-ASVAB.

Duration and Pacing

The ASVAB's duration varies based on the format used. It usually takes less time to finish the CAT-ASVAB than the paper version because it is adaptable. Candidates must effectively manage their time as each subtest in both forms has a time limit. As applicants must strike a balance between accuracy and speed, time management is an essential skill in this situation. Each subtest has a set time restriction that is intended to test a candidate's capacity to function under pressure—a critical ability in military settings.

The length of the ASVAB test varies depending on the format selected. Two main forms are offered for the ASVAB:

1. **CAT-ASVAB** (Computerized Adaptive Test): This test is administered at MEPS using a computer. The CAT-ASVAB comprises nine subgroups, 145 questions, and a time limit of 154 minutes.

2. **MET-site ASVAB** (Mobile Examination Test site ASVAB): This version of the exam is administered at multiple test locations throughout different cities and is used only for enrollment into the military services. The 225 questions on the MET-site ASVAB have a time limit of 149 minutes.

Scoring System

A vital component of the test is the ASVAB scoring system, which is intended to precisely evaluate a candidate's aptitude and suitability for military duty. Because the ASVAB does not punish erroneous responses, unlike many other standardized examinations, it deliberately encourages candidates to attempt every question. This method seeks to offer a thorough assessment of the test-taker's abilities and knowledge in a number of different areas.

The amount of questions answered correctly on a raw score is converted into standardized scores as part of the scoring procedure. After then, the results of these standardized tests are contrasted with a nationally representative sample of high school students' ASVAB scores. Contextualizing an individual's performance in relation to a larger group is aided by this comparison.

The Armed Forces Qualifying Test (AFQT) score, which is based on four important subtests — Word Knowledge, Mathematics Knowledge, Arithmetic Reasoning and Paragraph Comprehension — is essential to the ASVAB scoring system. The AFQT score indicates how a test-taker's score relates to the reference group and is expressed as a percentile ranking between 1 and 99. An AFQT score of 60, for example, indicates that the person performed on par with or better than 60% of the reference group.

A candidate's eligibility for recruitment in the US military is mostly dependent on their AFQT score. Minimum AFQT score standards are defined for each branch of the military and are subject to change depending on the demands of the service. In addition to making enlistment easier, a recruit with a higher AFQT score also has access to a wider variety of occupational opportunities and specializations.

Preparation and Practice

Being well-prepared is essential to getting a high ASVAB result. The first step in this procedure is to familiarize yourself with the content sections and format of the test. Test anxiety can be decreased and performance can be improved by being aware of the different question styles and topics addressed.

It is quite helpful to practice using example questions and to take extended practice exams. These test-taking drills give you an idea of how the test will flow and point out areas that require more research. Additionally, they support the development of test-taking techniques including time management and the capacity to rapidly identify the best responses.

Utilizing a variety of preparation tools in conjunction with consistent, focused study habits greatly raises the possibility of scoring highly on the ASVAB. It is advised that applicants plan ahead for adequate time and pursue their studies methodically.

Test Day Experience

The ASVAB exam day can be a demanding experience, therefore applicants should be well-prepared to get through this important stage. Being aware of the procedures and requirements on test day is crucial, regardless of whether you choose to take the computer-based CAT-ASVAB or the conventional paper-and-pencil version.

The Military Entrance Processing Station (MEPS) or the Military Entrance Test (MET), which is a satellite location, are often where candidates take the CAT-ASVAB. The test's digital style necessitates a basic understanding of computers. Because of the CAT-ASVAB's adaptive design, which modifies question difficulty based on test-taker responses, there may be an additional psychological pressure.

In order to finish each subtest in the allocated time on the paper version, applicants are frequently seated in a classroom-like environment. It is important to pay close attention to correctly filling out the answer sheets for the paper test.

Applicants must to be psychologically ready for a demanding examination setting. It is critical to maintain composure, self-assurance, and concentration. It's recommended that you eat a healthy breakfast and wear comfortable clothing to the test. Throughout the test, applicants should attentively study each question, use their time wisely, and keep in mind that it's preferable to guess than to leave a question unanswered.

Candidates can increase their chances of receiving a high score on the ASVAB and opening up doors for a lucrative military career by comprehending the scoring methodology, practicing extensively, and being well-prepared for the test day experience.

Post-Test Procedures

It is imperative that applicants comprehend the post-test procedures following their completion of the ASVAB. The benefit of taking the CAT-ASVAB is that results are available right away. Because of the computerized format's speedy processing, test-takers can get their results quickly after finishing the exam. The next steps in the enlisting process can be planned with the help of this instant feedback.

On the other hand, processing time for the paper form of the ASVAB, which is normally given in schools or at Military Entrance Processing Stations (MEPS), is lengthier. The human processing and assessment of the response sheets is the cause of this delay. Those who choose to apply on paper should be patient, evaluate their performance, and think about possible military careers during this time of waiting.

The results of the ASVAB, in any version, are crucial in establishing a candidate's eligibility for the US military. These ratings are more than simply numbers; they also show potential places for a candidate to fit within the military hierarchy. They assist in determining the candidates' strong and weak points and direct them toward positions where they have the most chance of succeeding.

Utilizing ASVAB Scores

ASVAB scores are used for purposes other than only being eligible for enlisting. These results are crucial in matching candidates with military careers that best suit their interests and skill set. Each military branch has distinct requirements for various roles. A higher ASVAB score frequently leads to additional options for employment in the military, enabling applicants to pursue positions that are more specialized and technically challenging.

Furthermore, some highly desirable military postings may only be awarded to applicants who receive scores significantly higher than the minimal qualifying score. This feature emphasizes how crucial it is to perform exceptionally well on the ASVAB in addition to passing it. A strong score has the potential to make all the difference in landing a dream job and have a big influence on a candidate's military career path.

Continuous Learning and Improvement

The ASVAB is an ongoing educational process. If they are not satisfied with their exam results, applicants have the option to retake it. One of the most important parts of the ASVAB procedure is this chance for improvement. It enables applicants to evaluate their study methods once more, pinpoint their areas of weakness, and address them before taking the test once more.

For individuals who want to raise their ASVAB results, it is strongly advised that they pursue ongoing education and skill development. This could entail looking for extra resources, such study guides or tuition, concentrating on particular subtests that require improvement, and using practice exams to gain experience and confidence.

It is also necessary to comprehend the policies surrounding the frequency of retests in order to retake the ASVAB. In order to properly arrange their preparation and retesting approach, candidates must be aware of the specified waiting periods between tries.

In conclusion, completing the ASVAB is a continuous learning and development process. It's a procedure that evaluates a candidate's present talents while also motivating them to advance and improve them. The final step in preparing applicants for a prosperous and fulfilling career in the military is this continuous process of learning and self-improvement.

SCORES AND INTERPRETATION OF RESULTS

Understanding the scores and interpreting the results of the Armed Services Vocational Aptitude Battery (ASVAB) is a crucial aspect of the examination process for anyone aspiring to join the U.S. military. The ASVAB is not just a test of knowledge; it's an assessment of potential and capability. The scores obtained in this test play a pivotal role in shaping the future of military candidates, influencing both their eligibility for enlistment and the range of occupational specialties available to them.

Understanding the meaning of their ASVAB results is the first step for applicants to have a successful military career. It's about realizing how these numbers, which represent their skills and abilities, might lead to a variety of chances inside the military context. In order to help candidates understand the ASVAB scoring system and make well-informed decisions on their military futures, this chapter attempts to demystify the system.

AFQT Score

The scores for the four subtests that make up the Armed Forces Qualification Test (AFQT) are: Word Knowledge, Arithmetic Reasoning, Mathematics Knowledge and Paragraph Comprehension. The basic eligibility for enrollment in the military is determined by this score, which is expressed as a percentile rating. A candidate may have more possibilities when it comes to potential military employment the better their AFQT score. In conclusion, the AFQT score serves as a candidate's entry point into the military and is more than simply a numerical value. It not only establishes a candidate's eligibility for recruitment but also shapes the course of their military career. Thus, candidates hoping to obtain their preferred position in the U.S. Armed Forces must prepare thoroughly for these four subtests.

Composite Scores

For individuals hoping to enlist in the US military, understanding composite scores on the ASVAB is essential since it has a direct impact on the variety of occupational specializations that are open to them. Different from the AFQT score, these composite scores—also called line scores—provide a more detailed picture of a candidate's aptitude in particular domains. Any potential service member must comprehend how these scores are determined and applied.

1. **Composition of Composite Scores**: The ASVAB's composite scores are produced by combining the results of several subtests. The individual subtests that are utilized to determine a composite score are determined by the knowledge and abilities pertinent to certain military jobs. For instance, subtests like General Science, Arithmetic Reasoning, Mathematics Knowledge, and Electronic Information may be used in a composite score for a technical profession.

2. **Branch-Specific Scores**: The Army, Navy, Air Force, Marine Corps, and Coast Guard are the five branches of the US military, and each utilizes a different set of composite scores. These ratings are customized for the particular requirements and positions in every branch. The Army, for example, employs composite scores for Mechanical Maintenance (MM), Electronics (EL), and Clerical (CL), among other categories.

3. **Preparing for Desired Composite Scores**: ASVAB preparation is frequently customized by candidates to increase scores in particular composite areas related to their intended military career path. Comprehending the subtests that contribute to every composite score is essential for focused preparation and study.

4. **Impact on Career Advancement**: Achieving high composite scores can influence future career growth and promotion chances within the military in addition to the original job placement. High scores in pertinent composite areas may be necessary for admission to several advanced training programs and leadership positions.

5. **Continuous Relevance**: Composite scores are still important in a service member's career and are frequently taken into account when promotions or unique assignments are being considered. They serve as an indicator of a service member's ability in crucial areas necessary to meet the various operational demands of the military.

To sum up, a military candidate's career route is significantly influenced by their composite scores on the ASVAB. They offer a thorough evaluation of a candidate's aptitudes in particular domains, which has a direct impact on the prospects offered by different military occupational specializations. For individuals seeking for specific roles in the U.S. Military, comprehending and concentrating on these scores can be a calculated strategy.

Retaking the ASVAB

Those who want to raise their ASVAB results in order to fulfill the minimum qualifying standards for military duty or to be considered for a particular position or program within the military, have the option to retake the exam. But candidates must be aware that there are guidelines and deadlines surrounding the ASVAB retake process.

1. **Eligibility for Retaking the ASVAB**: If an applicant is unhappy with their initial ASVAB results, they can usually retake the exam. This holds true for people looking to raise their scores in order to meet certain work requirements as well as those who have not achieved the minimal score needed to be enrolled.

2. **Waiting Periods**: To give candidates enough time to be ready for a retest, the military has instituted waiting periods in between ASVAB exams. One month following the initial test, the first retest can be taken. One month following the initial retest, a second one can be taken if needed. Every subsequent attempt at a retest must be separated by six months.

3. **Preparation for Retesting**: Those who are thinking about retaking the exam should make good use of the time they have beforehand. This could entail going over the areas in which they performed worse and concentrating on study resources that address these deficiencies.

4. **Impact of Retaking the ASVAB**: Whether a candidate's most recent score on the ASVAB is higher or lower than their previous score, it is their latest result that counts when they retake the test. As a result, before taking the test again, candidates must make sure they are more prepared.

5. **Limitations on Retests**: The ASVAB can be taken as many times as desired; however, repeated testing is not advised. Furthermore, certain recruiting stations might have their own restrictions or demands regarding retesting.

6. **Strategic Considerations**: Candidates who are getting close to the age requirement for military duty or who have a specific enlisting date in mind should carefully plan when they take their retest. With careful planning, individuals can make sure they have enough time to meet their goals without jeopardizing their plans to enlist.

7. **Consultation with Recruiters**: Military recruiters are a good resource for applicants to speak with before opting to retake the ASVAB. In addition to offering information on how to enhance scores based on the particular requirements of the desired military branch and career role, recruiters can offer insightful advise on whether a retest is required.

In conclusion, retaking the ASVAB is a feasible strategy for raising scores, but it needs to be carefully thought out and planned. In order to improve their chances of receiving higher scores on retakes, candidates should assess the advantages against the time and effort needed for preparation. They ought to take advantage of the waiting times as well.

SPECIFIC REQUIREMENTS FOR DIFFERENT MILITARY BRANCHES

The Armed Services Vocational Aptitude Battery, or ASVAB, is a crucial test for anybody hoping to enlist in the US military. There are specific minimum ASVAB score requirements for each branch of the military, which are important for both enrollment and to be eligible for certain military occupational specialties (MOS). Prospective service members must be aware of these standards in order to match their preparation and professional goals.

- **Army ASVAB Requirements**: Enlistment in the U.S. Army, which is renowned for offering a wide variety of occupational specialties, necessitates a minimum ASVAB score of 31. But this is only the entry-level need. Various ASVAB scores are required for different Army occupations, each with its own set of responsibilities and obstacles. For example, compared to other occupations, technical or intelligence responsibilities could require greater ratings. The Army takes a comprehensive approach to ASVAB scores, taking into account each candidate's potential and suitability for particular tasks.

- **Air Force ASVAB Requirements**: The Air Force sets a higher standard for its ASVAB criteria because of its emphasis on technical and aeronautical skills. The Armed Forces Qualification Test (AFQT) minimum score requirement is 31, but for candidates with a high school equivalency credential such as a GED, TASC, or HiSET, it rises to 65. Because of its emphasis on cutting-edge technology and sophisticated equipment, the Air Force has strict criteria, which calls for a staff with strong technical and analytical skills.

- **Coast Guard ASVAB Requirements**: The minimum ASVAB score required by the Coast Guard, which is well-known for its vital duties in maritime security and safety, is 40. This sector looks for people with a solid fundamental skill set because it frequently functions in difficult and demanding circumstances. The requirements are stricter for candidates with a high school equivalency degree; they must have at least 15 hours of college credit in addition to a minimum AFQT score of 50. The Coast Guard's dedication to having a highly qualified and educated personnel is demonstrated by this requirement.

- **Marine Corps ASVAB Requirements**: The Marine Corps, which is well-known for its exacting standards and exceptional standing, demands a score of at least 31 on the AFQT. This branch, which puts great emphasis on its adaptability and battle readiness, caps the number of GED enlistees at five percent annually. For those with a GED, a minimum score of 50 is needed. The Marine Corps prioritizes physical strength and mental toughness, which is reflected in their approach to ASVAB scores.
- **Navy ASVAB Requirements**: A minimum AFQT score of 31 is required by the Navy due to its wide diversity of operational conditions (26 is accepted in same instances). Candidates with a GED must have at least 50 college credit hours completed in order to be considered. The Navy needs people who can handle difficult marine and technology issues, as evidenced by the ASVAB criteria.

For those considering joining the military, it is essential to comprehend these ASVAB standards. Within each branch, higher ratings might lead to more specialized and coveted professions. For example, compared to other occupations, positions in technical maintenance, cybersecurity, or intelligence may demand higher ASVAB scores.

To sum up, the ASVAB plays a vital role in determining the future of military people. Candidates can increase their chances of not just joining the military but also landing a position that best suits their goals and skill set by learning the unique needs of each branch and tailoring their training accordingly.

CHAPTER 3 - EFFECTIVE STRATEGIES FOR ASVAB PREPARATION

OPTIMIZING YOUR STUDY PLAN

Starting the process of getting ready for the Armed Services Vocational Aptitude Battery, or ASVAB, is a big step on the path to becoming a successful soldier. The goal of this chapter, "Optimizing Your Study Plan," is to walk you through the process of designing a customized study plan that works for your unique schedule and learning preferences. You may make the most of your study time and raise your chances of getting a high ASVAB score by using the tactics that are described below.

Understanding the ASVAB Structure

One of the most important things you can do to get ready for the ASVAB is to get a thorough understanding of its structure. The Armed Services Vocational Aptitude Battery, or ASVAB, is a comprehensive exam that evaluates a broad variety of abilities and information relevant to different military positions. It consists of several smaller examinations, each concentrating on a distinct area, such as verbal, mathematical, technical, or spatial skills.

Every ASVAB subtest has a different format and set of questions. For instance, the Word Knowledge subtest assesses your vocabulary and word meaning comprehension, while the Arithmetic Reasoning subtest gauges your aptitude for handling simple arithmetic problems. It is important to comprehend the subtleties of each subtest so that you can choose which sections fit best with your strengths and which might be more difficult. To create a study regimen that is both effective and productive, it is necessary to possess this knowledge.

You can also improve your test-taking technique by being acquainted with the kinds of questions and the amount of time allocated for each subtest. Understanding the format, whether it be multiple-choice, fill-in-the-blank, or another kind, aids in mentally being ready for the type of approach and thought process that each part calls for. With a thorough understanding of the ASVAB's structure, you may prepare more effectively and feel less nervous on test day because you'll know exactly what to expect.

Assessment of Current Knowledge

To further optimize your study strategy, you should take a close look at your present knowledge in each of the different ASVAB subject areas. Either a diagnostic test or a series of practice ASVAB exams can be used to accomplish this. These diagnostic tools are made to closely resemble the format and content of the genuine ASVAB, giving you an accurate assessment of your present skill level.

It's crucial to try to replicate the real ASVAB exam conditions as much as you can when taking these practice exams. This entails respecting the deadlines and abstaining from outside assistance. After finished, a thorough study of your findings is essential. Keep a careful eye on the questions you answered right and, more crucially, the ones you answered incorrectly. You can identify some areas where you thrive and others where you might need to give more attention by using this study.

For example, you may find that, while your mechanical comprehension needs work, your mathematical knowledge is strong. This knowledge is quite helpful since it enables you to modify your study schedule to meet these particular requirements. Furthermore, knowing the causes of your poor responses—whether it's a misunderstanding, a misreading of the question, or a straightforward error—can offer further direction on how to organize your study sessions.

Setting Realistic Goals

One essential element of a successful study plan is the establishment of clear, achievable goals. The SMART criteria—Specific, Measurable, Attainable, Relevant, and Time-bound—should guide these objectives. You can greatly improve your motivation and focus by creating a clear path for your ASVAB preparation by making SMART goals.

Begin by establishing clear objectives for every ASVAB subtest. For instance, you may establish a goal to raise your score in the Electronics Information subtest by a specific percentage or point total if your initial assessment indicates that you need to improve. In order to monitor your progression toward achieving these objectives, make sure you can quantify these targets. This can entail taking practice exams frequently to track your score progress.

Achievable and reasonable goals are also essential. If too ambitious goals are not met, they may cause irritation and demotivation. Instead, strive for little, difficult but attainable gains through consistent work.

Relevance is yet another crucial component of your goals. Make sure that the objectives you create are closely related to your ultimate aim of performing well on the ASVAB. This entails concentrating on topics that are most relevant to the military positions you are considering.

Finally, you should set time-bound goals. You can stay motivated and on track by giving yourself deadlines to meet your goals. For example, you may set a goal to raise your score on a specific subtest within a month. This time-bound strategy makes sure that you are steadily advancing toward your objectives and becoming ready for the ASVAB.

Creating a Study Schedule

Creating a productive study plan is essential to preparing for the ASVAB successfully. It's important to establish a habit that blends seamlessly into your everyday life rather than merely scheduling time. Examine your present obligations to employment, education, family, and social life first. Determine your most attentive and productive moments. Are you an early riser or do you perform at your best in the evenings? Make your study schedule around these peak hours by using this understanding.

Make sure your study schedule is detailed and accurate. Instead of just putting in your study time for "in the afternoon," set specific times, like from 2:00 PM to 4:00 PM. This method creates a routine and lessens procrastination. Make sure your study sessions are long enough for you to fully absorb the information, but not so lengthy that you become distracted. Sessions lasting one to two hours are usually effective, however this can vary depending on the attention spans of each individual.

It's important to maintain balance. All of the ASVAB subtests should be covered in your study strategy, but not equally. Spend more time on the things that you find difficult, but don't forget to regularly evaluate your strong points. This well-rounded strategy guarantees thorough planning.

Include pauses in your itinerary. Frequent and brief breaks can assist sustain high levels of focus and stave off burnout. Engage in relaxing activities during these intervals, but stay away from distractions that could throw off your study schedule.

Finally, exercise disciplined flexibility. You might occasionally need to make schedule adjustments because life can be unpredictable. On the other hand, make an effort to make up for lost time and adhere to your plan precisely. Keeping up a consistent study regimen is crucial for achieving on the ASVAB and for long-term memory retention.

Focus on Weak Areas

While a comprehensive study is necessary, enhancing your total ASVAB score requires concentrating on your weak areas. Determine the subtests and particular themes where you performed poorly after your initial assessment. This targeted approach can help you organize your study time more effectively.

Make a strategy to deal with these weak points. Divide difficult subjects into smaller, more digestible chunks. Learning becomes more systematic and less intimidating with this split. Make use of a variety of resources to develop a comprehensive grasp of these topics. A alternative approach or explanation can occasionally clarify a confusing idea.

Include a variety of teaching methods. Try watching a lesson video, having a discussion about it with a study group, or consulting a tutor if reading about a concept isn't helping. Another effective technique to bolster your comprehension of a subject is to teach it to someone else.

Practice your weak regions' questions and problems on a regular basis. This exercise boosts confidence in addition to aiding with subject comprehension. Monitor your development in these areas. If you discover that your efforts aren't yielding the intended results, you might want to think about getting tutoring or other extra assistance.

Recall that raising your ASVAB score can help you considerably in your weakest areas. If you approach these areas with perseverance and patience, you will eventually transform your shortcomings into strengths.

Practice Tests

A vital component of efficient ASVAB preparation is doing timed, full-length practice exams. These drills accomplish a number of goals. First of all, they assist you in determining your present preparation level by pointing out both your advantages and disadvantages. You become used to the pressure of finishing the test in the allocated time by imitating the real exam setting. This is important for time management during the actual exam.

These practice exams should be incorporated into your study regimen on a regular basis. Your scores should rise as you get better at your preparation, and the amount of time it takes you to finish each section should also go down. This growth is an actual indicator of your increasing skill level.

It's crucial to carefully check over your answers, particularly the ones you didn't get right, after finishing each practice exam. It's just as crucial to comprehend why you made a mistake as it is to know the right response. Whether your blunders are the result of casual mistakes, conceptual misunderstandings, or problems with time management, this technique helps you find patterns in them.

Practice exams also aid in endurance strengthening. The ASVAB is a long exam, so being able to stay focused is essential. Your body and mind will become accustomed to withstanding the mental strain that such an exam entails with regular practice.

Review and Revise

To ensure long-term retention of material and to consolidate your learning, you must regularly evaluate and revise your work. This procedure is reviewing the content you have studied to strengthen your memory and comprehension. You can increase the depth of your conceptual understanding through effective revision, which will help you remember facts during the test more rapidly and accurately.

Writing a summary of the content in your own terms is an effective revising technique. This could be jotting down quick notes, making mind maps, or even imparting knowledge to another person. Recall and comprehension are improved when you summarize because it requires you to think critically and internalize the information.

Additionally useful are mnemonic devices, particularly for learning lists or sequences by heart. These can be associations, rhymes, or acronyms that help the material stick in the mind.

The principle of spaced repetition suggests gradually increasing the interval between consecutive revision sessions. This approach makes use of the psychological spacing effect, which states that increasing the frequency of material revisits enhances memory retention.

Staying Motivated and Positive

It's not only advised but imperative that you keep a positive outlook and stay motivated during your ASVAB preparation process. The ASVAB material can be challenging and even overwhelming to learn at times. To keep yourself motivated during each study session, consider setting small, achievable goals. These could be as easy as finishing a study session without interruptions, becoming better on a practice test, or even mastering a specific subject. Appreciate these tiny triumphs because they represent important turning points in your journey to achievement.

Making a system of rewards for yourself can help you stay motivated. This might be anything from organizing a quick get-together or activity after hitting a big goal to rewarding yourself with your favorite snack after a productive study session. These incentives act as a reminder of your accomplishments and diligence in addition to giving you something to look forward to.

Maintaining sight of your final goal is another essential component of motivation. Remember your initial motivation for taking the ASVAB. Recalling your ultimate objective can serve as a strong incentive, whether it's to challenge yourself, follow a certain military profession, or open up new opportunities. Imagine yourself succeeding and the career you have ahead of you. This vision can motivate you to prepare.

And it's very important to keep a good outlook. It's common to run into challenging material or to have days when your performance on practice exams isn't up to par. It's critical to maintain your optimism and try not to be too hard on yourself at these moments. Think back on your progress and the things you've already managed to do since starting your preparation. Keeping an optimistic outlook can not only increase the effectiveness of your study sessions but also lessen tension and anxiety.

Final Preparations

When the ASVAB test date approaches, it's critical to modify your study plan. Consolidating your information and boosting your confidence should be the goals of this prep period. Start by progressively lowering the level of difficulty in your study sessions. Instead than trying to learn something new, go over and reinforce what you already know. This can involve reviewing your notes, going over difficult subjects again, and doing a few easy practice questions.

Practice exams should be utilized less as an assessment tool and more as a revision aid in these last days. To maintain your abilities sharp, work through the questions; nevertheless, do not overburden yourself with new or difficult material. Now is the time to strengthen your trust in your knowledge rather than sow doubt with uncharted territory.

A crucial part of your last preparations should also include rest and relaxation. Ensure that you get adequate sleep, especially the night before the exam. A well-rested mind can remember details better and is more focused and attentive. Try to find peaceful pursuits to divert your attention from the test, such reading, gentle exercise, or quality time with loved ones.

Be cool and confident when it comes to test day. Have faith in your preparation and the acquired information. Recall that the ASVAB assesses not only your academic aptitude but also your tenacity and commitment. You're putting yourself in the greatest possible position to do well on the test by remaining composed, confident, and focused.

In summary, the latter phases of your ASVAB preparation are equally important for your mental and emotional health as they are for your academic health. You can succeed on the ASVAB by making the most of your study schedule, concentrating on revision, getting enough sleep, and keeping an optimistic and self-assured attitude. Your hard work and commitment to studying will help you not only get a good score but also build a strong base for your future military career. Recall that this voyage is evidence of your dedication and perseverance—attributes that will be invaluable to you in your military pursuits.

ESSENTIAL GUIDE FOR EXAM DAY

The day of the ASVAB test is the result of all your preparation, hard work, and dedication. This day has the power to determine how your military career develops in the future. As such, going into it with a well-thought-out plan is essential. The goal of this chapter is to give you useful and efficient guidance so that you can perform to the best of your abilities on test day.

1. **The night before the Exam** : The night before the exam is when the real preparing for the day starts. Getting a good night's sleep is crucial. To guarantee that your mind is rested and attentive, try to get 7-8 hours of good sleep. Steer clear of studying or cramming late at night as these activities can cause tension and exhaustion, both of which are detrimental. Prepare everything the night before the test. This entails assembling the required paperwork, such as identification and entry tickets, and verifying the list of items that are permitted and prohibited from being brought into the examination room. Arrange your clothing and include a small bag containing necessary items such as water, snacks, and additional pencils.

2. **Morning of the Exam**: Make sure you have a calm and focused routine for the morning before the exam. Start the day with a well-balanced breakfast that consists of healthy fats, carbohydrates, and protein. This will give you constant energy during the test. Steer clear of filling or strange foods that could make you uncomfortable. Allow enough time for yourself to travel to the testing location. Planning your departure time should take traffic, being lost, and parking into account. Being early can help you feel less anxious and allow you more time to unwind and be ready mentally.

3. **At the Exam Center**: After you get to the testing location, take some time to unwind and calm yourself. Relaxation techniques like deep breathing or meditation can help reduce anxiety. Discussing preparation materials or the exam with other applicants can lead to further anxiety and uncertainty. Observe the

instructions that the exam administrators have supplied carefully. Make sure you are aware of the regulations, particularly those pertaining to the usage of materials and calculators. Please don't hesitate to ask for clarification if something is unclear.

4. **During the Exam**: Spend some time attentively reading the instructions when the exam starts. Invest additional time in the sections that you find challenging to make the most of your time. When faced with a challenging question, try not to linger on it for too long. Make a note of it and move on, coming back to it later if time allows. Consider how comfortable you are physically. If you start to feel tense, take a moment to stretch or relax your muscles and adjust your seating. Remaining physically comfortable can lessen weariness and aid with focus.

5. **Breaks and Time Management**: Control is essential during the test. Watch the time, but don't allow it control how quickly you move. Avoid rushing and work methodically instead as this can result in thoughtless errors. Use the time you have left over after finishing a section to go over your responses, paying particular attention to areas where you are less confident. We'll go into more detail on efficient time management tactics in the upcoming chapter, giving you more tips and methods for completing the exam sections quickly.

6. **Post-Exam**: After the test is done, give yourself a time to celebrate your diligence and hard work. Succeeding on the ASVAB, regardless of the outcome, is a noteworthy achievement entirely. Post-exam analysis with other applicants should be avoided as it can cause unneeded anxiety and self-doubt.

The day of the ASVAB exam is a crucial turning point in your preparation for a career in the military. You may make sure that you approach the test in the greatest possible physical and mental condition by adhering to these instructions. Recall that your prior preparation will help you succeed. Have faith in your skills, maintain composure, and put out your best effort.

STRATEGIES FOR FIRST-TIME SUCCESS

It's a great objective to pass the ASVAB on your first try, but it takes a combination of mental toughness, strategic planning, and real-world knowledge. The goal of this chapter is to provide you with techniques that will help you pass the ASVAB on your first try, in addition to being practical.

Understanding the ASVAB's Unique Challenges
The ASVAB is not like other academic exams because it has a different set of questions. This all-encompassing test assesses a wide range of competencies, from verbal fluency to technical capabilities. The ASVAB is divided into sections that are meant to assess distinct skill sets. For instance, the Word Knowledge part covers more than just vocabulary recognition; it also covers subtleties in word usage and meaning. It calls on an acute command of the language and the capacity to recognize minute distinctions between words that are identical.

In a similar vein, the Mathematics Knowledge part covers more than just basic math. It covers a variety of mathematical ideas, including as algebra and geometry, and frequently calls for the application of theoretical understanding to real-world issues. This portion assesses your ability to reason logically and solve problems in addition to your mathematical knowledge.

Comprehending the unique characteristics of every segment is vital for proficient preparation. It's critical to tackle every part with a plan suited to its unique set of requirements. For example, rather than only memorizing formulas, one should concentrate on comprehending mechanical principles and physical laws when getting ready for the Mechanical Comprehension portion.

Developing a Targeted Study Approach
A focused study strategy is necessary for effective ASVAB preparation. Identifying your strengths and shortcomings through a thorough self-assessment is the first stage in this approach. Practice exams and diagnostic tests can help with this because they provide a clear image of the areas that need greater attention.

It's critical to devote more time and resources to improving your weakest areas after you've identified them. This does not imply, however, that you should totally disregard your advantages. The secret is to take a balanced strategy that builds on your strong points while strengthening your weaknesses.

In particular, practice exams are a useful tool. Along with acquainting you with the format of the exam, they also assist you with applying theoretical information in a setting like to an exam.

Effective Time Management

With each component of the ASVAB being timed, time management is an essential ability. It's critical to acquire the skills necessary to evaluate and respond to inquiries with speed and accuracy. This ability is especially crucial for areas like Paragraph Comprehension and Arithmetic Reasoning, where long passages or challenging problems might take a lot of time.

Practicing with timed tests is one of the finest ways to improve time management skills. These mock exams ought to replicate the real exam environment as much as feasible. You'll eventually gain an instinctive feel for timing, knowing how long to spend on each question and when to move on.

Accuracy and speed must be balanced delicately. While answering questions quickly can result in thoughtless errors, devoting too much effort to difficult questions can cut into the time allotted for subsequent questions. You'll be able to find the ideal balance with repeated practice, so you can finish each section in the allocated time without sacrificing precision.

It's important to know how to divide your time across portions if you want to manage your time well on the ASVAB. Based on the proportion of the overall exam time, use this helpful strategy to allocate your time:

1. **Arithmetic Reasoning (30% of your time)**: This section assesses your aptitude for math and problem-solving. Take a little longer to complete these tasks, particularly if they are complicated and call for several steps.
2. **Word Knowledge (15% of your time)**: Since this section is about recognizing and understanding words, it generally requires less time per question. Focus on quickly identifying the meaning of words.
3. **Paragraph Comprehension (15% of your time)**: Allocate a moderate amount of time to this section. While reading comprehension is important, the questions are usually straightforward.
4. **Mathematics Knowledge (20% of your time)**: This section involves high school-level math concepts. Allocate a significant portion of your time here, especially for questions that involve calculations and problem-solving.
5. **General Science (2,5% of your time)**: Questions in this section are generally fact-based and can be answered more quickly if you are well-prepared.
6. **Electronic Information (5% of your time)**: Like General Science, this section is more about recalling information, so it doesn't require as much time per question.
7. **Auto and Shop Information (2,5% of your time)**: This section tests specific knowledge, and if you're familiar with the content, you can move through these questions relatively quickly.
8. **Mechanical Comprehension (5% of your time)**: Allocate a moderate amount of time to understand and answer these questions, especially if you are less familiar with mechanical principles.
9. **Assembling Objects (5% of your time)**: This section assesses your ability to visualize spatial objects and understand how pieces fit together. While it may take some time to visually analyze each question, if you have a good spatial understanding, you can proceed relatively quickly. Allocate enough time to accurately visualize the object configurations before selecting your response.

Recall that these are only suggestions. Depending on your talents and limitations, the amount of time you actually spend on each part may change. The best method to determine how much time you need for each segment and modify your approach is to take practice exams.

Critical Thinking and Problem-Solving Skills

To perform well on the ASVAB, particularly in subjects like Mechanical Comprehension and Arithmetic Reasoning, one must enhance their critical thinking and problem-solving skills. With strategy and experience, these abilities can be cultivated and refined; they are not natural. Take up tasks that test your ability to reason logically and analytically to start. Logic games, brainteasers, and puzzles are great resources for honing these skills.

Instead of merely learning formulas, concentrate on comprehending the underlying principles when preparing for the ASVAB. For example, in Arithmetic Reasoning, comprehend the why and how of mathematical formulas rather than merely memorizing them. You will be able to apply these ideas to a wider range of problems—even ones that don't seem familiar—thanks to this greater understanding.

Problem decomposition exercises are another useful tactic. This entails dissecting intricate issues into smaller, easier-to-manage components. By breaking down a problem, you can address each part separately and reduce the overall difficulty of the problem. This method works especially well for the Mechanical Comprehension segment, where you could come across intricate machinery and systems. Clarity and understanding into a system's overall functioning can be obtained by comprehending the role that each component plays within it.

Practice several question and problem formats as well. Being asked a wide range of questions will improve your critical thinking and problem-solving skills in a number of situations. Frequent practice with ASVAB sample questions and tests can help you become comfortable with the format of the exam and develop a methodical and efficient approach to problem-solving in your brain.

Techniques for Memorization and Recall

It is imperative to develop efficient methods for memorizing and recall, particularly for areas such as Word Knowledge where a broad vocabulary is essential. Using mnemonic devices is one such strategy. Memory enhancers such as mnemonics make information simpler to remember by encoding it in a different way. You can make sentences, acronyms, or even tales that relate to the terms you need to remember. By utilizing your brain's innate ability to recognize patterns and tell stories, this method helps you remember knowledge.

Another effective memory aid is visualization. You can improve your memory power by associating the information you need to remember with mental pictures or scenarios. Consider seeing a term and its definition in a clear-cut situation. The image will be simpler to remember if it is more distinct and bright.

Another important memory strategy is association. Recalling new information becomes easier when it is connected to previously learned material in your memory. When learning a new phrase, for instance, attempt to correlate it with a term or idea that you already understand.

It is essential to regularly examine and repeat these approaches in addition to others. Particularly useful is spaced repetition, which involves reviewing material at progressively larger intervals. By utilizing the psychological spacing effect, this technique guarantees information retention over time.

Physical and Mental Preparation

Being mentally and physically prepared is essential to doing well on the ASVAB. Your physical well-being has a big influence on your mental clarity and focus. Prioritize keeping a healthy, well-balanced diet full of nutrients that promote brain health in the weeks before the test. Omega-3 fatty acids, vitamins, and antioxidant-rich foods are thought to enhance memory and cognitive function. Regular exercise is also very important. Exercise reduces stress and improves mental clarity in addition to strengthening the body. Walking and yoga are examples of mild exercise that can provide substantial advantages. Prioritize maintaining a regular workout schedule in the days before the exam.

Another essential component of physical preparation is getting enough sleep. Make sure you get enough sleep, particularly in the days before the test. Cognitive performance and memory consolidation are significantly impacted by sleep. A relaxed mind is more capable of critical thought, focus, and problem solving.

Just as crucial is mental preparedness. Have an optimistic outlook on the test. Use stress-reduction strategies like visualization, meditation, and deep breathing. You can approach the exam with a clear and focused mentality by using these tactics to help relax your mind and lessen worry.

Remain composed and optimistic on the day of the test. Refrain from last-minute cramming since it may be harmful and anxiety inducing. Trust your study abilities and approach the test with confidence. Keep in mind that your performance can be greatly impacted by your mental state, so remain composed and optimistic throughout the test.

Utilizing Practice Tests Effectively

Practice exams are an essential part of your study plan; they're not merely a way to be ready for the ASVAB. By providing you with a realistic exam experience, these tests aid in your adjustment to the exam's structure and time limits. Whenever you take a practice test, make every effort to simulate the exam setting. Set a timer, look for a peaceful area, and stay focused. By practicing this, you will be able to build the mental toughness that you will need on exam day.

The actual work starts once the practice test is finished. Examine each response, even the ones that are accurate. Determine the factors that make one response accurate while the others are not. Both your comprehension of the material and your test-taking abilities will increase as a result of this in-depth analysis. If you gave an incorrect response, consider what knowledge gaps or misconceptions you may have had. By engaging in this introspective activity, mistakes become worthwhile teaching moments.

Additionally, monitor your development over time. Are you doing better in some areas? Do the same kinds of errors keep happening? With this continual assessment, you may modify your study plan and focus your efforts where they are most required.

Seeking Feedback and Guidance

Although studying on your own is crucial, getting outside advice and criticism can greatly improve your ASVAB readiness. Having conversations with peers provides a cooperative learning environment. Study sessions in groups might be quite helpful. Talking with people about a subject might help you grasp it better and introduce you to new viewpoints and methods of approaching problems.

Make use of study groups and internet forums as well. You can communicate with other ASVAB candidates using these platforms. It can be quite helpful to ask questions, share resources and experiences, and give advice. Recall that learning is frequently more successful when it is a shared experience.

Building Endurance for the Test

The extensive and varied components of the ASVAB test not only measure knowledge but also endurance. Developing endurance is essential to keeping your concentration and productivity during the test. Start by progressively extending the duration of your study sessions in order to accomplish this. Start with shorter, more manageable study periods and gradually extend them. By gradually increasing, you can assist your body and mind get used to prolonged periods of focus, just like in an exam.

Include lengthy practice exams in your study regimen. These are essential for developing stamina because they mimic the actual test situation. By recognizing when you begin to feel tired, this practice also helps you come up with counterstrategies like taking quick mental pauses or switching to a different kind of question.

Consider including some physical exercise in your routine as well. Frequent physical exercise, such jogging or even simple stretches, can greatly enhance mental clarity and focus. Exercise improves mood and energy levels, boosts blood flow to the brain, and lowers stress—all of which are helpful while getting ready for a challenging exam like the ASVAB.

Lastly, never forget how crucial it is to keep up a nutritious diet and drink plenty of water. Eating a balanced diet gives you the energy you need to focus for extended periods of time, and drinking enough water keeps your brain functioning at its best.

Conclusion: A Holistic Approach for First-Time Success

Being successful on your first try at the ASVAB requires a lot of work. It necessitates a comprehensive strategy that extends beyond academic training. It's only the beginning to combine a solid academic foundation with efficient test-taking techniques. To ensure success, being mentally and physically prepared is equally crucial.

A positive mindset must be developed in order to be mentally prepared. Trust your abilities and the effort you have invested in becoming ready. To handle any pre-test nervousness, use stress-reduction methods like deep breathing, meditation, or visualization. During the test, having a clear and collected head can greatly improve your memory and decision-making skills.

Developing an adaptable mentality is also essential. Throughout the test, be ready to face unforeseen obstacles; have solutions ready for them. This could be as simple as pausing to refocus if you see that your attention is wandering or ignoring questions that take too much time and coming back to them later.

Always keep in mind that studying for the ASVAB involves more than just getting a good score. They are intended to provide a solid basis for your upcoming military career. You will benefit much beyond the test from the abilities, routines, and attitudes you form during this time, as they will help you meet the difficulties of military training and duty. You will position yourself for success on the test and in your future profession if you view the ASVAB as a chance to hone and demonstrate these traits.

CHAPTER 4 - ASVAB EXAM SECTIONS

ARITHMETIC REASONING

One of the most important parts of the Armed Services Vocational Aptitude Battery (ASVAB), which acts as a starting point for a career in the US military, is Arithmetic Reasoning. This crucial ASVAB portion assesses a candidate's ability in basic mathematics, a core skill set required for many military tasks and responsibilities as well as the test itself.

Arithmetic reasoning goes beyond numbers and computations in the context of military operations. It represents the capacity to swiftly comprehend, evaluate, and resolve issues that frequently arise in real-world situations. Making quick, correct decisions is essential in a variety of military contexts, from field tactics and strategy creation to supply chain management and logistics.

Therefore, the Arithmetic Reasoning portion of the ASVAB assesses an individual's ability to apply mathematical ideas in real-world scenarios as well as their aptitude with numbers. It evaluates a candidate's proficiency with reading, interpreting, and solving word problems—a test of their ability to reason logically and make wise decisions under duress.

This section's significance also stems from its function in establishing a candidate's eligibility for particular military occupational specialties (MOS). In the military, a great score in arithmetic reasoning can lead to a variety of opportunities, including specialized and technical jobs requiring a strong background in mathematics.

Fundamentally, there is more to the Arithmetic Reasoning part than just assessing computation skills. Rather, it goes further, evaluating the candidates' ability to comprehend and solve mathematical problems that are presented in a narrative style. Like little case studies, each of these puzzles presents a distinct situation that calls for the logical application of mathematical concepts. The questions are designed to simulate the kind of rapid, precise computation and judgment required in the military.

This section's tasks range in complexity from simple computations to intricate multi-step procedures. Applicants may come across situations where they must use fundamental algebraic and geometric concepts or compute timings, distances, and quantities. The variety of questions guarantees a thorough evaluation of a candidate's mathematical proficiency.

This section is unique in that it emphasizes contextual problem-solving. The problems are designed so that in order to find a solution, candidates must first recognize the pertinent mathematical principles and then apply them correctly. This method assesses understanding and critical thinking capabilities in addition to numerical aptitude. It's not only about the arithmetic knowledge that applicants possess; it's also about how well they use it.

Furthermore, the part on Arithmetic Reasoning demonstrates the usefulness of mathematics in military operations. Processing numerical data quickly and properly is essential when calculating the trajectory of an artillery round, working out how much fuel a mission requires, or allocating resources. Therefore, this portion functions as a reliable indicator of a candidate's capacity to meet the mathematical requirements of military duty.

To put it simply, the Arithmetic Reasoning portion of the ASVAB involves more than just math. It is a thorough assessment of a candidate's aptitude for deciphering, reasoning through, and solving mathematical puzzles in a way that is representative of how these abilities are actually used in the military. In addition to testing applicants' mathematical prowess, this portion assesses their ability to apply that knowledge in practical settings, a skill that is critical to the military.

Types of Questions Typically Encountered in the Arithmetic Reasoning Section

- **Basic Operations**: The basic operations of addition, subtraction, multiplication, and division are tested in these problems. Although they are simple, they demand quickness and accuracy. For instance, candidates may be required to figure out how much the things cost in total or how much money was left over after a transaction.

- **Word Problems**: Word problems make up a sizable component of the Arithmetic Reasoning section. These questions ask candidates to extract and process numerical data from real-world circumstances. For example, a question can require the candidate to calculate the quantities dispersed in a scenario where supplies are allocated to different units.

- **Fractions and Decimals**: This category of questions involves working with decimals and fractions. It is possible that candidates will be required to compute fractional quantities or convert fractions to decimals and vice versa. These questions test your proficiency with numbers in a range of formats and require a firm grasp of basic mathematical concepts.

- **Ratios and Proportions**: The candidate's comprehension of and proficiency with ratios and proportions is evaluated by these questions. They frequently take the shape of issues that call for comparing numbers or figuring out how much of one thing is related to another.

- **Percentages**: A critical ability assessed in this area is the ability to calculate and understand percentages. Calculating discounts, interest rates, and the percentage rise or decrease in quantities are some examples of the questions that may be asked.

- **Basic Algebra**: The Arithmetic Reasoning portion contains fundamental algebra questions, although it does not place a strong emphasis on intricate algebraic ideas. These usually entail figuring out unknown numbers by utilizing algebraic expressions or solving straightforward equations.

- **Estimation**: Examinees may come across questions where estimates will suffice in lieu of exact calculations. The ability to quickly and reasonably estimate is put to the test in these problems; this is a useful skill in many military applications that occur in real life.
- **Sequencing and Patterns**: Certain questions may ask candidates to determine the following number in a series or comprehend the reasoning behind a numerical pattern. These questions may also incorporate sequences or patterns.

Every one of these question kinds calls for a different strategy and level of comprehension. Knowing how to apply mathematical operations to solve real-world issues is just as important for success in the Arithmetic Reasoning section as mastering mathematical processes themselves. Quick and accurate mathematical reasoning can be critical to operational planning and decision-making in many military professions, thus this talent is necessary.

Strategic Approaches

- **Key Terms**: Analyzing each component of the problem is essential in mathematical thinking, especially for phrases that denote certain operations (such as addition or subtraction). Seek out essential terms like "less than," "subtract," or "reduce" in the case of subtraction, and "multiplied by," "of," or "triple" in the case of multiplication. Find these essential terms first in order to comprehend the necessary steps, and then solve the equation.
- **Interpreting Numbers**: Pay close attention to all of the numbers in the text. Sort these statistics, make a distinction between the ones that pertain to the issue at hand and the ones that could be inserted to deceive you. The order of the numerals is important to consider. For instance, it is only helpful to identify a 5 and an 8 in a problem if you can accurately determine their sequence. For example, the computations 8−5 and 5−8 produce different values and may have a major effect on your test scores.
- **Understanding Paragraph Structure**: In mathematical reasoning, paragraph form is essential. For instance, a physics problem will be organized differently than a fundamental algebra problem; physics problems usually require some kind of movement (such as a bike, train, or skateboard), whereas a basic math problem can be organized in a number of ways. First, take note of the structure and context of the paragraph in order to identify the kind of issue you are working with. After that, combine the important words and figures to create a concise, understandable equation.
- **Fundamental Techniques**: It's important to read the question thoroughly, identify all the important components, and cross out any unimportant information in order to prepare for the Arithmetic Reasoning segment of the ASVAB. Word problems frequently contain irrelevant material intended to divert your attention because they are verbose compared to the equations or functions themselves.

When working on these issues, make a list of all the pertinent details, create a workable equation, and solve it. Feel free to move on to questions you find simpler if you're unsure about a particular one, especially if it's a paper-and-pencil test. The more difficult questions can always be revisited at a later date. To score higher, utilize patience and logical thinking whichever the format of the test. Make sure you have a solid understanding of the most important mathematical concepts while you prepare.

Fundamental Arithmetic Concepts
Types of Numbers

- **Whole Numbers**: These are numbers starting from 0 and increasing infinitely without any fractional parts, such as 0, 1, 2, 3, and so on.
- **Counting Numbers**: Similar to whole numbers but excluding 0, as 0 cannot be counted. These are also known as natural numbers and include 1, 2, 3, etc.
- **Integers**: This set encompasses all positive counting numbers, their negative counterparts, and 0, for example, -3, -2, -1, 0, 1, 2, 3, etc. Positive integers are above 0, while negative integers fall below 0.
- **Natural Numbers**: These positive whole numbers, which go on forever like 1, 2, 3, and so on, are also known as

counting numbers.

- **Rational Numbers**: Any number expressible as a fraction of two integers falls into this category. This includes fractions like 7/5, -3/4, and 11/923. Whole numbers also fit here as they can be represented over 1 (e.g., 5/1). Non-repeating decimals are included too, such as 2.8, which is 28/10.
- **Irrational Numbers**: These numbers cannot be expressed as a ratio of two integers. Examples include the square root of 5 and π.
- **Real Numbers**: Encompassing all rational and irrational numbers, real numbers cover every point on a number line.
- **Imaginary Numbers**: Any number in the form of "ai", where "a" is a real number and "i" is the square root of -1. For instance, the square root of -4 can be expressed as 2i.
- **Complex Numbers**: These are numbers in the form "a+bi", where "a" and "b" are real numbers, such as 2+5i.

Special Numbers of Importance

- **Prime Numbers**: Numbers divisible only by themselves and one, like 2, 3, 5, 7, 11, etc. The number 1 is not a prime number as it is only divisible by itself.
- **Even Numbers**: Numbers divisible by 2 without a remainder, such as 0, 2, 4, 6, 8, etc.
- **Odd Numbers**: Numbers that leave a remainder of 1 when divided by 2, like 1, 3, 5, 7, 9, etc.
- **Factor**: An integer that divides another integer evenly. For example, 2 is a factor of 10, as 2 multiplied by 5 equals 10.
- **Multiple**: The result of multiplying two or more integers. For instance, 10 is a multiple of 2 because 2 times 5 equals 10.
- **Consecutive Numbers**: Number sets that increase by one. For example, five consecutive integers are 3, 4, 5, 6, 7, and five consecutive even numbers are 2, 4, 6, 8, 10.

The Four Basic Operations

- **Addition**: The process of adding two or more numbers to get a sum.
- **Subtraction**: The process of deducting one number from another to get a difference.
- **Multiplication**: The act of multiplying two numbers to get a product.
- **Division**: Dividing one number by another to obtain a quotient.

Fundamental Numerical Properties

When utilizing the four main mathematical operations, it is essential to comprehend the fundamental characteristics of numbers. The Associative, Commutative, and Distributive Properties are the cornerstones of many different approaches to problem-solving.

- **Commutative Property of Addition**: The order of adding numbers does not affect the sum:
  4+6+3=13 is equivalent to 6+3+4=13
- **Commutative Property of Multiplication**: The order of multiplying numbers does not affect the product:
  4·6·3=72 is equivalent to 6·3·4=72
- **Associative Property of Addition**: The grouping of numbers to be added does not affect the sum:
  (4+6)+3=13 is equivalent to 4+(6+3)=13
- **Associative Property of Multiplication**: The grouping of numbers to be multiplied does not affect the product:
  (4×6)×3=72 is equivalent to 4×(6×3)=72
- **Distributive Property**: To multiply a number by a sum inside parentheses, multiply it by each addend within the parentheses and then sum these products:
  3(4+6)=3·4+3·6=12+18=30

This property implies distributing the number outside the parentheses across all numbers inside. It also allows for factoring out common elements from an expression. For instance:

3y+9y2

Using the distributive property, we can factor out 3y:

$3y(1+3y)$

- **Identity Properties**: In addition, there is a specific number that, when added to any number, leaves it unchanged. This number is 0, known as the Additive Identity. Similarly, in multiplication, multiplying any number by 1 leaves it unchanged, making 1 the Multiplicative Identity.
- **Inverse Operations**: There is an inverse operation for every mathematical operation, which flips the result. Subtraction flips addition, and vice versa. Division undoes multiplication, and vice versa. Similarly, squaring and getting the square root of an integer are inverse operations.
- **Closed and Open Systems**: Under certain operations, certain sets of numbers stay within the set. For example, combining any two odd numbers consistently yields an even number, hence the result stays in the even number range. Addition and multiplication close this set. On the other hand, the set of odd numbers is open under division since, in many cases, dividing one odd number by another yields a fraction that lies outside of the set.

Operation Rules

Comprehending certain principles can be quite helpful while performing arithmetic computations, especially when confirming the correctness of your answers. With this knowledge, you can determine whether an answer is obviously wrong or implausible very fast.

Even and Odd Numbers

- **Addition**: An even number is always obtained by adding two even numbers. Summing two odd numbers also yields an even number. However, combining an odd number with an even number always results in an odd number:
  $4+4=8$
  $7+9=16$
  $5+8=13$
- **Subtraction**: This property is consistent in subtraction:
  $6-4=2$ (even)
  $9-5=4$ (even)
  $8-5=3$ (odd)
- **Multiplication**: Multiplying two even numbers always gives an even number:
  $10 \cdot 4=40$
  Multiplying an even number with an odd number also results in an even number:
  $6 \cdot 7=42$
  However, multiplying two odd numbers produces an odd number:
  $9 \cdot 7=63$
- **Division**: If a number divides evenly by its divisor, the even/odd characteristic remains as in multiplication. If not, there's a remainder, making the quotient a fraction, and thus neither even nor odd.

Positive and Negative Numbers

On a numerical scale, numbers located to the right of zero exhibit positive growth, whereas those situated to the left experience negative reduction. Numbers grow larger in either direction, but their value only increases to the right and decreases to the left.

Think of positive and negative numbers as bank account balances when working with them. On the number line, making a deposit causes you to move right (positive). When you take out cash, use a debit card, or write checks, you are deducting money and going to the left on the number line. When you overdraw beyond zero, you enter negative numbers. These numbers increase in size but are denoted by a negative symbol (-), which means you have an overdraft.

Note: Numbers without a negative sign are assumed to be positive.

- **Addition and Subtraction**
  Subtracting a negative number equates to adding a positive number:
  $4-(-4)=4+4=8$
  Adding two negative numbers always results in a negative number:
  $-6+(-10)=-16$

Adding a positive number to a negative number yields a positive result if the positive number is larger than the absolute value of the negative number; otherwise, the result is negative:

$-6+9=3$

- **Multiplication and Division**
  Multiplying two positive integers always results in a positive integer:

  $7 \cdot 7 = 49$

  Multiplying two negative integers yields a positive integer:

  $-7 \cdot -7 = 49$

  But multiplying a positive integer with a negative integer results in a negative integer:

  $-7 \cdot 7 = -49$

  In division, the sign rules are the same as in multiplication. However, if the integer doesn't divide evenly by its divisor, the outcome is a fraction, not an integer.

Absolute value

The numerical separation between a number and zero on the number line can be used to understand the idea of absolute value. Typically, this is shown by encircling the number with vertical line symbols, like thus: $|\ |$. For example, $|-7| = 7$ denotes that -7 has an absolute value of 7. This is true since seven is a positive number, and that is the absolute value of -7.

Examine the formula $|x-6|=4$. In this instance, x may be two or ten. This is due to the fact that there are two possible solutions to the absolute value equation.

We frequently utilize a piecewise function, which necessitates two different equations, to express absolute values. Consider the basic equation $y=|x|$. The equation $y=x$ still holds true if x is a positive value. If x is negative, on the other hand, we negate the negative to turn it into a positive, creating the equation $y=-x$.

The two distinct equations for $y=|x|$ are:
- $y=x$ for $x>0$
- $y=-x$ for $x<0$

The graph's left and right sides are linear in their graphical depiction, but the graph as a whole is not. For this reason, one equation is insufficient. The graphs of the first and second equations are located on the right and left, respectively.

In conclusion, as can be shown in the instance of absolute value, a piecewise function is one in which the result of the function is defined using multiple equations.

Multiplication as a Form of Addition Repeated

Think of multiplication as an accumulation of additions.

For instance, in the expression $3 \cdot 5$, we are essentially adding 3 five times:

$3+3+3+3+3=15$

This is the same as the multiplication fact we learn in elementary school.

Division as Even Distribution

Division is the process of evenly distributing a quantity. It's like sharing a certain number of items among a group.

For example, if we have six oranges and want to share them between three people, we divide 6 by 3:

$6 \div 3 = 2$

Each person receives two oranges.

Understanding Prime Numbers

Each number can be written as the product of one and itself, for example, $6=6 \cdot 1$ and $7=7 \cdot 1$. All integers divide evenly by one and by themselves. On the other hand, a prime number can only be divided by one and itself; it has no other divisors.

The first ten prime numbers are: 2, 5, 11, 13, 17, 19, 23, 29, 31, and 37.

Composite Numbers

An integer that is divisible by all numbers except one and itself and is not categorized as a prime is called a composite number.

For instance, 18 is divisible by 1, 2, 3, 6, 9, and 18.

Identifying Factors

The numbers that divide an integer evenly are called its factors. The integer is the product of these components multiplied in specific combinations. For instance, the number 18 has multiple factors:

$18 = 18 \cdot 1$

$18 = 9 \cdot 2$

$18 = 6 \cdot 3$

Determining the Greatest Common Factor

Consider two numbers, such as 36 and 48, which share common factors. The largest of these is the greatest common factor.

The factors of 36 are 1,2,3,4,6,9,12,18, and 36.

The factors of 48 are 1,2,3,4,6,8,12,16,24, and 48.

The common factors are 1,2,3,4,6, and 12. The greatest common factor is 12.

Prime Factorization Explained

Dividing a number into its prime factors is known as prime factorization. For instance, think about the number 30. We employ its prime elements, which are 2, 3, and 5, to obtain 30:

$30 \div 5 = 6$

$6 \div 3 = 2$

$2 \div 2 = 1$

We used 5 once, 3 once, and 2 once, giving us the prime factorization $2 \cdot 3 \cdot 5$, which equals 30.

Multiples and Their Significance

An integer is a multiple of itself when it is multiplied by another integer. For example, since these factors add up to 18, 18, is a multiple of its factors.

Finding the Least Common Multiple

Consider two numbers, such as 6 and 15. Their multiples are:

Multiples of 6 are 6,12,18,24,30,36,42,48,54,60...

Multiples of 15 are 15,30,45,60,75...

The common multiples are 30 and 60. The least common multiple is 30, useful in fraction addition for finding a common denominator.

Understanding Remainders

A remainder is what's left after dividing one number by another. For example, in $17 \div 6$, 6 divides into 17 twice, leaving a remainder of 5.

Rules for Divisibility

Divisibility rules help identify which integers divide a number evenly. These rules for numbers 2 through 10 include:

2—All even numbers are divisible by 2. If a number's final digit divides by two, it is even.

3— A whole number is divisible by four if its final two digits are as well. Example: 21 has digits 2 and 1, and 2 +1 =3, which is divisible by three.

4—If the last two digits of a number are divisible by 4, then the number is divisible by 4.

5—Numbers ending in 0 or 5 are divisible by 5.

6—A number divisible by both 2 and 3 is divisible by 6.

7— Take the last digit, double it, then deduct it from the total. The initial number is also divisible by 7 if the outcome is. For example, with 49, double 9 to get 18, subtract from 4 to get -14, which is divisible by 7.

8—If the last three digits of a number are divisible by 8, then the number is divisible by 8.

9—Like the rule for 3, if the sum of a number's digits is divisible by 9, then the number is divisible by 9. Example: 72 has digits adding up to 9, which is divisible by 9.

10—Numbers ending in 0 are divisible by 10.

Fractions

Parts of a whole can be expressed as fractions, which are usually expressed as numerator/denominator. Here, the total parts are shown by the bottom number, and the portion of the entire is indicated by the top number. For example: Tim would have eaten 2/6 of the oranges in a basket if he had eaten two of the six oranges.

Types of Fractions

- **Mixed Number**: A complete integer and a fractional component are both included in this kind of fraction. Mike eating all six oranges from one basket and then two more from another, for instance, might be represented as a mixed fraction: 1 6/2
- **Improper Fraction**: The top number in an incorrect fraction is greater than the bottom number. Add the bottom number to the top number after multiplying the bottom number by the entire number to turn a mixed fraction into an improper fraction. The original bottom number is retained, and the new top number creates the incorrect fraction. Divide the bottom number by the top number to turn an incorrect fraction into a mixed number. The quotient is the total number, while the remainder becomes the new top number.
- **Reciprocal Fraction**: To find the reciprocal of a fraction, flip the numbers at the top and bottom. 6/2 is the reciprocal of 2/6.

Equivalent Fractions

Although they could look different, equivalent fractions have the same value. For instance, 3/9 is equal to 1/3. You may be required to identify a fraction with a bottom number of 9 that is equal to 1/3 in a given problem. This relationship is used to find the missing top number:

1/3=top number/9

Cross-multiplying 9 and 1 gives 9, and dividing 9 by 3 gives 3. Hence, the top number is 3. This results in the equivalent fraction of 3/9.

Simplifying and Reducing to Lowest Terms

Reducing fractions to their most basic form is the act of simplifying them. Consider these fractions:

3/9, 6/18, 9/27

They all simplify to 1/3. To simplify 3/9, factor both numbers:

$(3 \cdot 1)/(3 \cdot 3)$

The 3s cancel out, leaving the simplified fraction: 1/3

Adding and Subtracting Fractions

Convert equivalent fractions having a common bottom number in order to add or subtract fractions with distinct bottom numbers. Subtract or add to the top numbers after that.

Find the least common multiple (LCM), divide the original bottom number by the LCM, and then multiply the quotient by the original top number to obtain the new top number.

For instance, in 1/4 + 3/20, the LCM is 20, so 1/4 must be converted to an equivalent fraction with 20 as its bottom number.

Divide 4 into 20 to get 5, then multiply 5 by 1 for the new top number: 5/20

Multiplication of Fractions

Multiply the top numbers to get a new top number, and the bottom numbers for a new bottom number. Simplify the outcome if required.

For instance, $3/8 \cdot 4/5=12/40$ Put simply, this is: 3/10 Fractional Division

Multiplying the first fraction by the second's reciprocal allows you to divide fractions.

Division of Fractions

Divide fractions by multiplying the first fraction by the reciprocal of the second.

Example: $3/7 \div 4/9=3/7 \cdot 9/4$

Decimals

Similar to fractions, decimals can be used to express portions of a whole; however, the denominator of a decimal always has a base of 10, which is not shown explicitly.

Let's look at the decimal 0.035. The final digit on the right determines the power of 10 that serves as the denominator in this case. A digit to the right of the decimal point, for example, indicates that the denominator is 10 (10^1), two digits indicate that it is 100 (10^2), three digits show that it is 1,000 (10^3), and so forth.

Hence, the fraction 35/1,000 can be used to represent the decimal 0.035. The place values for typical decimal points are broken down as follows:

- Ones: 1
- Tenths: 0.2
- Hundredths: 0.03
- Thousandths: 0.004
- Ten-Thousandths: 0.0002

The fundamental operations on decimals can be performed using the same concepts as those on whole numbers; however, it is important to note where the decimal point is placed in the final solution. This is how you handle that:

Addition and Subtraction

The decimal points should be vertically aligned while adding or subtracting. For the number of decimal places to be equal, you might need to add zeros to the right of the integers. The result's decimal point ought to be situated immediately beneath the other decimal points. Think about including 3.3 and 14.42, for example.

Place the decimal point precisely under the other two, add a zero to 3.3, align the decimal points, and carry out the column addition as normal.

14.42 +
 3.30 =
17.72

Now, try subtracting 2.42 from 18.6.

Add a zero to 18.6, align the decimal points, subtract as usual, and place the decimal point directly under the other two.

18.60 -
 2.42 =
16.18

Multiplication

Multiplying decimals involves two steps:

1. Disregard the decimal points and multiply as usual.
2. Decimal places in the original figures should be counted. To guarantee that there are an equal number of decimal places in the result, add a decimal point.

For example, multiply 0.06 by 2.1. There are three decimal places in total.

2.1 x 0.06 = 0.126

Now try multiplying 1.64 by 0.053.

1.64 x 0.053 = 0.08692

Ignoring the decimals, the answer is 8692, but we need five decimal places, so we add a zero to the left of the 8.

Division

For dividing decimals:

1. Shift the decimal points. To convert a decimal to a whole number, move it to the right in the divisor and the dividend, respectively.
2. In the quotient, place the decimal point exactly above where it appears in the dividend.
3. Divide as usual, keeping your numbers in columns.

For example, divide 1.8 by 0.3:

0.3:1.8

Shift the decimal point one place to the right:

3:18

Divide according to normal, increasing the dividend by zeros if needed.

To perfect arithmetic reasoning, one must comprehend and practice these operations with decimals, particularly in situations when accuracy and precision are critical, such as the ASVAB.

Exponents and Roots

Inverse operations are represented by these ideas. Raising a number to a given power, or multiplying it by itself a predetermined number of times, is what exponents do. However, a number that results in the number that appears beneath the root sign when multiplied by itself is called a root. This is similar to how division and multiplication are connected but different. Let's examine it.

Exponents

The number of times a number to be multiplied by itself is indicated by its exponent. This process is known as exponentiation.

3^4 means we multiply three by itself four times: $3\times3\times3\times3=81$.

Exponents, also known as powers, can be positive, negative, or even fractional, which we'll cover in the "Roots" section.

An exponent that is positive indicates how many times a number may be multiplied by itself.

7^3 equates to: $7\times7\times7$

A negative exponent represents how many times 1 is divided by the number raised to the exponent.

7^{-3} translates to: $1/(7\times7\times7)$

Rules for Working with Exponents

Remember these key rules when simplifying and evaluating expressions with exponents:

When a number or variable is multiplied by itself, add the exponents.

Basic rule 1: $a^m \cdot a^n = a^{(m+n)}$

Example: $3^2 \cdot 3^4 = 3^{(2+4)} = 3^6$

When a number or variable is divided by itself, subtract the exponents.

Basic rule 2: $a^m \div a^n = a^{(m-n)}$

Example: $4^6 \div 4^3 = 4^{(6-3)} = 4^3$

When a number or variable is raised to a power and then to another power, multiply the exponents.

Basic rule 3: $(a^m)^n = a^{(m\times n)}$

Example: $(3^3)^2 = 3^{(3\times2)} = 3^6$

Radicals

Radicals, also known as roots, are often represented with the $\sqrt{}$ symbol, known as the radical sign, root symbol, radix, or surd. They can also appear as fractional exponents, such as:

$x^{(1/2)}$, which is equivalent to $\sqrt{x}$.

$36^{(1/2)} = \sqrt{36} = 6$

$z^{(3/2)} = (z^3)^{(1/2)} = \sqrt{(z^3)}$

The term inside the radical sign is called the radicand.

Radicals show how many times a number is multiplied by itself to get the specified number; they work in the opposite way as exponents. A radical is represented by the $\sqrt{}$ symbol and, if it is more than 2, may contain an index, which is a number in the small corner. The most popular radical, the square root, finds the number that, when squared, equals the input.

Fractions can also be used as the exponent in the expression of radicals. The denominator, like the index, shows how many times the base number needs to be multiplied by itself to be equal to the base number.

The inferred index of $\sqrt{16}$ is not displayed when calculating a number's square root. Comparable to using 1/2 as the exponent is this.

$\sqrt{16} = 16^{(1/2)} = 4$

Logarithms

Logarithms may not frequently appear in the ASVAB pencil-and-paper test, but they are more common in the CAT-

ASVAB. Logarithms, a variant of exponents, are simpler than they seem.

The expression log2(16) poses the question:

"How many times must you multiply 2 (the 'base') by itself to get 16?" The answer is four.

Hence, log2(16) = 4 (Interpreted as: "The log base 2 of 16 is 4.")

Its exponential equivalent is: $2^4 = 16$

In equations involving logarithms, you often need to find the value of a variable. For instance:

Find x in:

log3(2x+1) = log3(9x)

Both sides of the equation have the same base (3), meaning the arguments (terms inside the parentheses) must be equal. Therefore, you solve:

2x+1 = 9x

which yields:

x = 1/7

Scientific Notation

In scientific notation, a number is represented as a power of ten multiplied by a decimal number between 1 and 10. When discussing very large or small numbers, this notation comes in handy. For example, 24,678,000,000 is a bit much, but $2.4678 \cdot 10^{10}$, the scientific notation, makes it easier to handle.

Factorials

The factorial, denoted by the exclamation point (!), instructs us to multiply a counting number by each whole number less than it, down to one.

For example, 5!, read as "five factorial", is:

$5 \cdot 4 \cdot 3 \cdot 2 \cdot 1$

$20 \cdot 3 \cdot 2 \cdot 1$

$60 \cdot 2 \cdot 1$

120

Here, five is multiplied by each whole number less than itself, down to one.

Measurement

The metric system, which is widely used in most nations, and the U.S. Customary system, which is unique to the United States, are the two main generally used methods of measurement. However, because many imported goods and some domestic goods employ metric measurements, the metric system is also used in the United States.

U.S. Customary System

For length, the inch is the fundamental unit. Other units include:

- 1 foot = 12 inches
- 1 yard = 3 feet or 36 inches
- 1 mile = 5,280 feet or 1,760 yards

In terms of volume, the fluid ounce is the basic unit. Additional units are:

- 1 cup = 8 fluid ounces
- 1 pint = 2 cups or 16 fluid ounces
- 1 quart = 2 pints or 32 fluid ounces
- 1 gallon = 4 quarts or 128 fluid ounces

For weight, the ounce is the standard unit. Other units are:

- 1 pound = 16 ounces
- 1 ton = 2,000 pounds

Metric System

The metric system employs various prefixes, each acting as a multiplier. Common prefixes include:

- kilo- — multiplied by 1,000
- hecto- — multiplied by 100
- deka- — multiplied by 10
- deci- — multiplied by 0.1
- centi- — multiplied by 0.01
- milli- — multiplied by 0.001

For length, the meter (m) is the basic unit. Other units are:

- 1 kilometer (km) = 1,000 m
- 1 dekameter (dam) = 10 m
- 1 centimeter (cm) = 0.01 m
- 1 millimeter (mm) = 0.001 m

In volume, the liter (L) is the primary unit. Other units include:

- 1 kiloliter (kL) = 1,000 L
- 1 centiliter (cL) = 0.01 L
- 1 milliliter (mL) = 0.001 L
- 1 cubic centimeter (cc or cm3) = 1 mL

For weight (or mass), the gram (g) is the basic unit. Other units are:

- 1 kilogram (kg) = 1,000 g
- 1 centigram (cg) = 0.01 g
- 1 milligram (mg) = 0.001 g

Converting Between Systems

While not essential for the test, understanding some basic conversions between the metric and U.S. Customary systems can be helpful:

- 1 inch = 25.4 millimeters = 2.54 centimeters
- 1 foot = 30.5 centimeters
- 1 meter = 39.37 inches = 3.28 feet
- 1 cup = 237 milliliters = 0.236 liter
- 1 quart = 946 milliliters = 0.946 liter
- 1 pound = 454 grams
- 1 kilogram = 1,000 grams = 2.2 pounds

Geometry Fundamentals

Geometry may not be a major focus of the ASVAB Arithmetic Reasoning Test, but it is still helpful to grasp these basic ideas and how they are calculated.

- **Perimeter**: The entire distance encircling a shape is its perimeter. Calculating it involves summing the lengths of all sides, or for a circle, using the formula $C = \pi \cdot d$, where C represents the circumference, π is approximately 3.14, and d stands for the diameter.
- **Area**: The area represents the space within a two-dimensional shape. For instance, the area a carpet covers on the floor, or the area of a wall needing paint. Different shapes have specific formulas for calculating area:
  - Square: $A = s^2$, where s is the side's length.
  - Rectangle: $A = l \cdot w$, with l as length and w as width.
  - Triangle: $A = \frac{1}{2} b \cdot h$, where b is the base and h is the height.
  - Circle: $A = \pi \cdot r^2$, with π around 3.14 and r as the radius.

- **Volume**: Volume measures the space within a three-dimensional shape, like the liquid in a cup or concrete in a basement. There is a distinct formula for calculating volume in each shape:
  - Rectangular prism: V=lwh, where l stands for length, w for width, and h for height.
  - Sphere: $V=4/3\pi \cdot r^3$, with π around 3.14 and r as the radius.

Data Analysis
Average, Mean, Median, and Mode
These are central tendency measures, describing data set characteristics.
Consider a class of 10 students with math exam scores:
64, 75, 92, 83, 87, 90, 88, 91, 93, 95
The average is the sum of all scores divided by the number of students.
For our example, the average score is:
(64+75+92+83+87+90+88+91+93+95)÷10=86.8
Average and mean are synonymous, both representing the typical score.
In an ordered set of data, the median is the middle number. When dealing with an odd number of data elements, count equally from both ends to determine the middle. The median of an even number is the mean of its two center values.
In our example, the median is the average of the 5th and 6th scores (87 and 90), which is 88.5.
Scores that occur the most frequently are called modes. In our data, 88 appears most often, making it the mode.

Other Data Concepts
- **Outlier**: An outlier is a single data point that stands out from the rest. It's sometimes excluded from calculations due to its extreme value.
- **Spread/Dispersion**: These terms describe how data points are distributed around the mean. Low values indicate data points close to the mean, suggesting consistency.
- **Range**: What separates the highest and lowest data values is called the range.
- **Variance**: Variance measures how much data points deviate from the mean. A large variance suggests data points that are dispersed widely.
- **Standard Deviation**: This provides an additional measure of the dispersion of the data; it is the variance squared.
- **Quartile**: Quartiles divide data into four equal parts. The first quartile includes the lowest 25% of data, the second is the median, and the third includes the lowest 75%.
- **Interquartile Range**: This represents the variation between the first and third quartiles, with an emphasis on the data's middle 50% range.

Probability
The entire set of possible outcomes of a given event, referred to as the sample space, determines the probability of an event occurring. Examine the following experiment: two coin flips. For this experiment, the sample space consists of HH, HT, TH, and TT. The coin has a one in four chance of showing tails twice.
1/4 or 25%
Like in the coin flip example, probabilities might be dependent or independent. Consider a situation where there are three balls in a bag: two green, one orange, and one purple. The likelihood of drawing a certain color after removing one ball, noting its color, and then not putting it back in the bag is dependent on the color of the removed ball. For example, the likelihood of drawing another green ball after the first one is as follows:
1/3 or 33%.

Concepts in Probability
- **Single Event**: One or more outcomes are included in an event. For example, there are three methods to roll a dice and hope to land on an odd number: 1, 3, or 5. When an odd number is rolled, the desired event is fulfilled by these three results (1, 3, 5).
- **Favorable Outcome**: A successful result satisfies a predetermined requirement. Since rolling an odd number is the condition in the case above, it would be advantageous to land on 1, 3, or 5. On the other hand, rolling a 2, 4,

or 6 would not be good.

- **Complement**: The results that don't fit the favorable parameters are all part of the complement of an event. If an odd number were rolled, the complement would be 2, 4, and 6.
- **Multiple Events**: The likelihood of multiple distinct events is occasionally sought after. For instance, given a regular deck of cards, what is the likelihood of drawing a queen and subsequently a jack? Alternatively put, what is the likelihood that if you draw just one card, it will be a jack or a queen?
- **Conditional Probability**: This is the likelihood that an event will transpire given the occurrence of an earlier event. What is the likelihood of drawing a white sock after drawing a black sock, for instance, if you had two black socks and two white socks? Initially, drawing the black sock modifies the pool of candidates for the second sock.
- **Mutually Exclusive Events**: These are the kinds of things that can't happen all at once. One can draw a card, for instance, and it can be either an ace or a king, but not both at once. So drawing an ace and drawing a king is unpossible.
- **Mutually Inclusive Events**: These things can happen at the same time. It is conceivable to draw a card in a card game that is both a ten and a heart, for instance. Drawing a heart and drawing a ten are mutually inclusive events. They may occur simultaneously.

Key Skills for ASVAB Arithmetic Mastery

To perform well on the ASVAB Arithmetic Reasoning Test, one must become proficient in a few key mathematical methods. Your capacity to solve problems will significantly increase if you grasp and put these basic concepts into practice.

Understanding the Order of Operations

The mathematical order of operations determines which operations are performed in what order within an expression. Orders (powers and roots), Brackets, Multiplication, Division, Subtraction and Addition is a helpful acronym in this context.

Consider this approach:

1. Start by solving expressions within brackets.
2. Next, address any powers or roots.
3. Next, take on any division or multiplication as it comes up, working your way from left to right.
4. Finally, address addition or subtraction, again working from left to right.

Ratios and Proportions

Ratios represent the relationship between two quantities. For example, if a basket contains three bananas and four apples, the ratio of bananas to apples is 3 to 4.

Ratios can be expressed in various ways:

- Using a colon: 3:4
- As fractions: 3/4
- As a percentage: three out of seven fruits are bananas, so approximately 43% are bananas
- As decimals: 0.43 of the fruits are bananas

The proportions show if the ratio stays the same as the quantities vary. For instance, we multiply both values by the same factor if we want to keep the banana to apple ratio of 3:4 in a larger fruit basket. Therefore, 3:4 and 9:12 are proportionate.

Inverse Proportions

If raising one causes a proportionate drop in the other, then two quantities are inversely proportional. For example, if you are traveling at 40 mph and it takes you 45 minutes to get to your destination, driving at 80 mph will only take you 22.5 minutes. Travel time decreases proportionately with increasing speed.

Rates in Mathematics

Rates are used to describe relationships between different quantities, such as speed, time, and distance. The formula for calculating distance is $d = rt$, where d is distance, r is rate, and t is time.

Rates also apply to financial contexts, like calculating interest. The formula for simple interest is: $FV = P(1 + nr)$, where

FV is the future value, P is the principal amount, r is the interest rate, and n is the number of periods.

Percentage

A percentage is a subset of one out of every 100. If you have 100 objects, for example, and 40 of them are of one type and 60 of another, then 40% of your goods are of the first type. For example, if there are 100 fruits in a fruit basket and 40 of the fruits are bananas and 60 are grapes, then 40% of the fruits are bananas.

Converting Fractions to Percentages

When the total isn't 100, we adjust the fraction so its denominator is 100, similar to creating an equivalent fraction. If there are 80 fruits, with 25 bananas and 55 grapes, we convert 25/80 to a percentage.

First, divide 80 into 100 to get 1.25, then multiply 1.25 by 25 to get 31.25. The fraction becomes 31.25/100.

Thus, we can say 31.25% of the fruits are bananas.

The Proportion Method

In the ASVAB Mathematics Knowledge section, many percentage problems can be solved using proportions:

percent/100 = part/whole

For example: What percentage of 25 is 7?

Let "x" represent the unknown percentage.

Here, 7 is the part, and 25 is the whole.

The equation becomes:

x/100 = 7/25

Cross-multiplying gives:

25x = 700

700:25 = 28

x = 28

Calculating Percent Change

Use the proportion method for complex percentage problems. For example: A phone was $450, down from $600. What's the percent decrease?

First, find the price drop:

600 - 450 = 150

The percent decrease, x, is:

x/100 = 150/600

150:600 = 0.25

Solving for x gives a 25% decrease.

Converting Fractions to Percentages or Decimals

Decimals, fractions, and percentages all indicate portions of an entire. For example:

1/100 is 1% or 0.01.

1/2 is 50% or 0.5.

ASVAB often involves converting between these forms. A fraction can be converted to a percentage by adding the % symbol, multiplying by 100, then dividing the numerator by the denominator.

For 1/2:

1 ÷ 2 = 0.5

0.5 x 100 = 50%

50% is the percentage form of 1/2.

To convert 50% back to a fraction:

Write 50% as 50/100.

Reduce to 1/2.

Sequences

A series of integers that follow a pattern is called a sequence. For example, even numbers form a sequence starting with 2, increasing by 2: {2, 4, 6, 8...}

Another sequence could be doubling the previous number and adding two, like:

2n + 2, starting with 1: {1, 4, 10, 22...}

Sequence Definitions

Arithmetic growth: A sequence where each number differs from the previous by a constant. For example, 3, 7, 11, 15, 19... is arithmetic, adding 4 each time.

Common difference: the arithmetic sequence's constant difference. It is four in the case above.

Recursion: A sequence where each number depends on the previous ones. Starting with 1, 2, __, add the two preceding numbers:

1, 2, 3 (1+2), 5 (2+3), 8 (3+5), 13 (5+8)...

WORD KNOWLEDGE

The ASVAB's Word Knowledge part is more than just a vocabulary test; it serves as a starting point for learning about language and communication, two essential military skills. This chapter covers the main ideas in this section and offers successful strategies.

The purpose of the Word Knowledge test is to evaluate your comprehension of word meanings through context and synonyms. This section focuses on comprehending the subtleties of language rather than just memorization of vocabulary. It's about the significance of words in various settings and how they are employed in different contexts.

Effective communication is essential in the military. An order, report, or directive contains words that have meaning. Misunderstandings may result in ineffectiveness or, worse, serious mistakes. Therefore, having a large vocabulary is crucial for communicating ideas clearly and precisely.

Strategies for Enhancing Vocabulary

The combination of extensive reading and contextual learning is a potent tactic in the process of improving one's vocabulary for the ASVAB. This method involves more than just coming across new terms—it involves submerging oneself in a multitude of situations that give these words life.

Reading a wide range of materials is necessary to increase your vocabulary. Every writing genre and style has its own lexicon and usage. For example, military publications introduce you to military jargon and technical terminology that is exclusive to the armed forces and is necessary to comprehend and communicate in a military setting. On the other hand, reading historical books can take you to different times and introduce you to vocabulary that may not be common but is essential to comprehending the complexity and context of the past.

Fiction offers a distinct flavor thanks to its intricate storylines and character dialogue. It introduces you to idioms, inventive word usage, and colloquial vocabulary that you might not find in more formal books. Fiction's ability to place words in emotionally charged situations is what makes it so beautiful and intriguing for readers to learn from.

Contextual learning solidifies your comprehension of new terms while reading exposes you to them. It entails observing words in action, including how they are employed in phrases, the nuances they convey in various settings, and the minute variations in meaning that can drastically alter the entire tone of a conversation.

For example, the term "charge" in a military journal could mean an attack or assault, while in a historical record, it might mean a feudal duty. It could be used in a dialogue in fiction to imply command or haste. Despite its simplicity, this term has a variety of meanings and weights depending on the situation.

Acknowledging the function of words in expressing emotion and tone is another aspect of contextual learning. For instance, figuring out the meaning of terms like "slim" and "scrawny" can be quite important for determining the tone of a text or conversation. In the Word Knowledge component of the ASVAB, where a word's meaning might change depending on its context, this level of comprehension is essential.

Integrate reading and contextual learning strategies to get the most out of this tactic. When you read and come across new words, pause to consider how they are used in that particular context. Jot down and evaluate the sentences or paragraphs that contain these terms. Make an effort to employ these terms in your own phrases, changing their meaning to suit various situations.

Use these new words in conversations and writing assignments as well. Engaging in active vocabulary use helps you remember terms better and improves your ability to use them effectively in various contexts.

Practice with Synonyms and Antonyms

It's important to have a firm understanding of synonyms and antonyms because the Word Knowledge part of the ASVAB often assesses your mastery of these concepts. This exercise goes beyond simply learning word pairings; it also requires exploring the finer points of language and realizing how small changes in meaning may change a word's entire context.

Making and reviewing lists of frequently misunderstood terms is a useful way to improve your knowledge of synonyms and antonyms. In addition to the terms themselves, these lists ought to provide definitions and instances of how the words are used in phrases. Think about terms like "malevolent" and "benevolent," for example. Despite having a similar sound, they have quite different meanings. An entry in a list could resemble this:

- Benevolent: Kind and generous.
    - Example: Her benevolent nature was evident in her volunteer work at the shelter.
- Malevolent: Possessing or displaying a desire to harm other people.
    - Example: The villain's malevolent intentions were clear from his menacing words.

By going over and adding to this list on a regular basis, you will eventually develop a mental library of terms, definitions, and opposites.

Finding synonyms and antonyms in a variety of literature that you read is another useful tactic. Anything from fiction novels to news items could be used for this. Observe how words with similar or opposite meanings are employed in various situations as you read. This exercise aids in your comprehension of the words' meanings as well as their implications and minute distinctions.

Reviewing consistently is essential. Allocate a specific period of time every day to review your word lists and drills. Self-assessment is another useful tool for tracking your development. You might look up a word's definition and attempt to remember it, or you could notice a term and attempt to come up with an antonym or synonym for it. By practicing active recall, you improve your memory and vocabulary comprehension.

Candidates are typically examined on two sorts of questions in the ASVAB Word Knowledge section: comprehending words' literal meanings and figuring out how they are used in particular circumstances. This dual approach assesses a candidate's vocabulary breadth as well as their practical application of the knowledge.

Direct Definition Questions

These are simple but difficult questions since they demand a precise grasp of the meaning of each term. For instance, a query might ask for the definition that is closest to a word like "Prolific" from a list of possibilities. Here, finding the synonym that most closely like the supplied word is crucial. "Prolific" in this context refers to the state of being very inventive or "productive".

It is essential to have a solid fundamental vocabulary in order to perform well on these questions. Reading frequently and being exposed to a variety of language sources can be quite beneficial in this regard. For example, reading the word "Prolific" in a variety of contexts can help you become more familiar with its definition and application.

Contextual Usage Questions

These tests evaluate your ability to deduce a word's meaning from its context in a sentence. Here, knowing how the word works in a certain context is more important than knowing its precise dictionary definition. Take this line, for instance: "Despite her cursory glance, Jane noticed the error in the report." "Cursory" in this sense denotes a brief or cursory inspection, which is necessary to grasp the broader meaning of the statement.

Focus on word usage in many contexts and hone your reading comprehension abilities to appropriately solve these challenges. This expands your vocabulary and strengthens your capacity to infer meanings of words you are unfamiliar with.

Now let's explore some real-world instances to better understand these ideas:

1. Direct Definition Example:

- Word: "Tenacious"
- Question: "Tenacious most nearly means ____."
- Options: persistent, weak, indifferent, rapid
- Correct Answer: persistent, as "tenacious" refers to being firm or holding fast.

2. Contextual Usage Example:

- Sentence: "Her tenacious pursuit of knowledge impressed her teachers."
- Question: "In this context, 'tenacious' most nearly means _____."
- Options: uninterested, fleeting, determined, casual
- Correct Answer: determined, as the sentence implies a strong and persistent effort in seeking knowledge.

Candidates can greatly enhance their performance in the Word Knowledge part of the ASVAB by comprehending these two main question patterns and practicing with real-world examples. Remember that the keys to success in this important exam section are to increase your vocabulary and use it contextually.

Prefixes, Suffixes, and Root Words: Decoding Vocabulary

Exploring the domains of prefixes, suffixes, and root words further is like discovering a gold mine of linguistic information. This comprehension is a lifetime skill that improves comprehension and communication, not only for the Word Knowledge portion of the ASVAB.

Prefixes

Prefixes are those tiny, important pieces at the start of words that have the power to completely change the meaning of the original term. They work similarly to keys to open various nuances of meaning. For example, the prefix "pre-" denotes "before." When used with a word like "determine," it becomes "predetermine," changing its meaning to "making a decision in advance." Some typical prefixes are as follows:

- "inter-" (between), as in "interact" or "intermediate"
- "super-" (above), used in "superior" or "supernatural"
- "trans-" (across), found in "transport" or "transcontinental"
- "auto-" (self), as in "autobiography" or "automatic"
- "hyper-" (over), used in "hyperactive" or "hypersensitive"

Suffixes

Suffixes can alter a word's grammatical classification as well as its meaning when they are added to the end of root words. Say you take a verb like "operate" and add the suffix "-tion" to make it a noun called "operation." This morphological shift is essential to successfully comprehending and utilizing language. Some more often used suffixes are as follows:

- "-ment" (action or process), as in "development" or "agreement"
- "-ive" (having the nature of), found in "creative" or "active"
- "-ous" (full of), as in "glorious" or "dangerous"
- "-ity" (quality of), used in "equality" or "ability"
- "-al" (relating to), as in "natural" or "functional"

Root Words

Words develop from their root words, which might have prefixes, suffixes, or both. Understanding root words well can be very helpful in understanding the meanings of more difficult words. As an illustration, the Latin root "scrib" or "script" signifies "to write." Many English words, including "describe" (to write about), "manuscript" (written by hand), and "inscription" (something written into), have their roots in this root.

Other noteworthy root words are:

- "Port" (carry), seen in "transport" (carry across) or "import" (carry into)
- "Graph" (write), as in "autograph" (self-written) or "biography" (life writing)
- "Therm" (heat), used in "thermometer" (measure of heat) or "thermal" (related to heat)

The ASVAB's Word Knowledge portion offers you the chance to improve your language skills, which are essential for a successful military career, in addition to testing your present vocabulary. You can greatly increase your score on this crucial ASVAB exam by realizing the value of language in communication, using efficient learning techniques, and practicing frequently. Recall that every phrase you learn will get you one step closer to realizing your dreams of joining the military.

PARAGRAPH COMPREHENSION

The ASVAB's Paragraph Comprehension component assesses a candidate's ability to critically evaluate and analyze written information in addition to reading comprehension. With the goal of giving you a deeper knowledge of this subject, this chapter will teach you the tools and techniques you need to excel in understanding complicated texts—a critical talent in both military and civilian situations.

1. **Identifying Main Ideas**: It's critical to identify the main idea or theme of a paragraph. This ability entails figuring out the main idea around which the text's details center. It's about getting the main idea of the paragraph, which usually means reading past the opening and closing words to get the entire picture.

2. **Inferring Meaning**: Your ability to interpret inferences and read between the lines is frequently tested on the ASVAB. This ability is essential in circumstances where you must make inferences from the available facts even while it isn't explicitly stated. It entails examining the text to infer implied meanings and objectives that are not explicitly stated.

3. **Evaluating Arguments**: This ability entails evaluating a text's arguments' validity and strength critically. It involves analyzing the reasoning behind claims, comprehending the supporting data, and deciding whether the arguments are sound, cogent, or defective.

Understanding Vocabulary in Context: Your ability to correctly infer a word's meaning from its context is evaluated in this section. The way a word is employed in a phrase or paragraph can give it a different meaning, and this portion evaluates your ability to discern these subtleties.

Strategies for Enhancing Comprehension Skills

1. **Active Reading**: Make reading an interactive activity rather than a passive one. Make predictions, pose questions, and connect the text's ideas to your own knowledge or experiences to actively engage with it. This method aids in improving knowledge retention and comprehension.

2. **Summarizing and Paraphrasing**: After reading a paragraph, try describing it in your own words. This method helps you retain the key ideas and helps you cement your understanding. Another measure of your paraphrasing skills is how well you can reword the text without changing its original meaning.

3. **Practice with Diverse Materials**: Reading a wide variety of texts, including fiction, narrative essays, and technical manuals, can greatly improve your comprehension of different topics and writing styles. A more varied set of comprehension skills is facilitated by the introduction of distinct structures, vocabulary, and ways of expressing ideas in each genre.

4. **Develop Critical Thinking**: Make it a habit to assess the text critically. Examine the author's goals, the target audience, and the potency of the descriptions or arguments. This exercise helps with text comprehension as well as the development of a critical attitude, which is beneficial in many facets of life, particularly when making decisions as a member of the armed forces.

Tips for the Exam

1. **Skim Before Reading**: To start, rapidly scan the paragraph to get a sense of its general theme and organization. This first synopsis lays the groundwork for more targeted and effective reading. When reading a paragraph carefully, it might be helpful to quickly grasp its overall theme, tone, and structure as this can help you better appreciate the finer nuances.

2. **Look for Keywords**: Look for terms that are essential to understanding the paragraph's core theme as you read. These could be titles, times, locations, technical phrases, or any other words that make sense in the situation. These terms can be quite helpful in providing proper answers to inquiries and are frequently used as anchors for comprehending the main idea.

3. **Manage Time Effectively**: During the test, time management skills are essential. When responding to the questions, make good use of your time. It's best to move on and come back to the subject later, if time permits, rather than spending too much time on it if you find yourself stuck. By using this strategy, you can be sure that you will have enough time to answer every question and increase your chances of receiving a higher score.

4. **Answer Based on the Text**: Make sure that the material in the paragraph serves as the exclusive basis for

your responses. Refrain from allowing personal ideas or outside knowledge to color your answers. Not your general knowledge or opinions, but your ability to understand and evaluate the presented text is what the ASVAB assesses.

Practice consistently is the key to success in the paragraph comprehension section. It is really beneficial to practice using sample questions and texts. These sample exams help you build a steady rhythm and successful study plan for the real exam in addition to acquainting you with the structure and kinds of questions you'll face.

It is easier to adjust to various writing styles and complexity when you practice with a range of texts. It is advantageous to incorporate items that test your comprehension abilities and force you to adjust and get better. Furthermore, going over your responses—especially the ones that were off—allows you to identify areas that require further attention and can help you avoid frequent traps.

By implementing these study techniques, you will improve your reading comprehension and become more competent when it comes to answering the ASVAB's Paragraph Comprehension part. Recall that regular practice improves your general analytical and interpretive abilities, which are crucial for your future military career, in addition to helping you get ready for the test.

Application in Exam and Beyond

The abilities developed by paragraph comprehension are not just useful on the ASVAB; they are also necessary for good decision-making and communication in everyday life and military operations. In the military, where precise understanding might have serious repercussions, the capacity to swiftly comprehend, evaluate, and react to written commands or reports is essential.

To sum up, achieving success in the ASVAB's Paragraph Comprehension portion necessitates a combination of attentive reading, analytical thinking, and varied reading strategies. By honing these abilities, you'll not only increase your chances of passing the ASVAB but also build a solid basis for critical thinking and effective communication in the military and beyond.

MATHEMATICS KNOWLEDGE

One of the most important parts of the ASVAB is the Mathematics Knowledge section, which assesses your understanding of algebraic and geometrical concepts. This chapter attempts to give a thorough grasp of what to anticipate in this section of the test as well as practical preparation tips.

You will be presented with 16 questions in the computerized CAT-ASVAB format, and you will have 20 minutes to answer them. On the other hand, the paper-and-pencil version has 25 questions and gives you 24 minutes to do it. These topics need a combination of computational and analytical skills and range in difficulty from simple word problems to sophisticated mathematical issues.

While fundamental arithmetic is not the main focus of this part, a strong foundation in these skills is essential to successfully navigating the algebraic and geometric obstacles that are provided. Because they serve as the foundation for more complex mathematical problem-solving, it is therefore wise to review and strengthen your arithmetic reasoning skills. This chapter and the study guide that goes with it are meant to help you navigate the complexities of the Mathematics Knowledge segment so that you are well-prepared for this important part of the ASVAB exam.

Algebra

One of the most important algebraic skills is the ability to manipulate algebraic expressions. These expressions combine mathematical operations, constants (fixed numbers), and variables (symbols for unknown quantities), but they noticeably lack an equal sign. When an expression has an inequality or equal sign, it is called an equation.

Algebraic Expressions: The Fundamentals

Simple single terms and sophisticated combinations of numerous terms are both possible in algebraic expressions. Algebraic expressions such as $24t$, $7x \cdot x + 6$, or $(x+4)(x-3)$ are examples. Every expression is a different combination of variables, constants, and operations that together produce a mathematical statement that does not resolve into an equality or inequality.

Terms: The Core Components

The constituent components that make up an algebraic expression are called terms. They may be products of variables and constants raised to a power, or they could be constants with plus or minus signs between them. For example, the terms r^2, $-7r$, and 8 occur in the formula r^2-7r+8.

Combining Terms: Streamlining Expressions

Combining terms can often simplify algebraic expressions. In this procedure, like terms—that is, terms with the same variable raised to the same power—are merged. Terms like $9x$ and $6x$, or $8y^3$, y^3, and $10y^3$, for instance, are similar and can be combined.

Consider the expression $6x^2+9x-3x^2+10+3x+x^2$. To simplify, group like terms: $6x^2-3x^2+x^2+9x+3x+10$. Then combine these like terms to get $4x^2+12x+10$.

Adding and Subtracting Terms

Adding and subtracting terms in algebra is simple. For constants, elementary arithmetic applies. When working with words that have variables, make sure the phrases are similar, and then modify the variable component by adding or removing the coefficients. For instance, $19x^2$ is produced by adding $15x^2$ and $4x^2$.

Multiplying and Dividing Terms

Algebraic multiplication and division don't require similar words. For instance, to multiply $8x^2y$ by $4x^3y^3$, multiply the constants (8 and 4) first, then combine the variables into one term ($32x^5y^4$) by applying the laws of exponents to the variables.

Types of Expressions

Expressions are categorized based on their number of terms:

- **Monomials**: Single-term expressions, such as $3x^3$ or $4xy^2z$.
- **Binomials**: Two-term expressions, like x^2-z^2 or $8x-5$.
- **Polynomials**: Expressions with multiple terms, such as $3x^2-4x+6$ or x^3+4x^2-6x+9. Polynomials can involve addition, subtraction, multiplication, and division (excluding division by variables).

Simplifying and Evaluating Expressions
Distributing

One essential algebraic principle that helps to simplify statements is the distributive property. Each term included in a bracket must be multiplied by the term outside of it. The formula is $a(b + c) = ab + ac$.

For example, consider the expression $4(x + 6)$. To distribute, multiply 4 by each term inside the brackets:

- $4 * x + 4 * 6$
- $4x + 24$

The expression is now simpler to work with in subsequent computations thanks to this simplification.

Factoring

The process of disassembling a complicated phrase into smaller parts, or factors, is known as factoring. It is the opposite of expanding and comes in handy when figuring out equations.

Consider the polynomial $9x + 20 - x^2$. We need to find two values that sum up to -9 and multiply to 20 in order to factor it. We require two values that, when put together, equal the coefficient of the x term (in this example, -9), and when multiplied, equal the constant term (20). The pairs (1, 20), (2, 10), (4, 5), and their inverses are a few examples of pairs that multiply to 20. Additionally, these figures must total up to -9. The only pair in our set that adds up to nine is (-5, -4). We construct two binomials using these integers. Our discovered numbers will represent the constant component of each binomial, and x will be its variable element. Consequently, (x - 5) and (x - 4) result. The numbers -5 and -4 fit this criterion.

- $(x - 5)(x - 4)$

These are the factors of the polynomial.

Solving Polynomial Equations

Finding the values of the variables that make an equation true is the first step in solving polynomial equations. This frequently calls for solving for the variable and setting the polynomial equal to zero.

Using the factored polynomial $(x - 5)(x - 4) = 0$, we find the roots by setting each factor equal to zero:
- $x - 5 = 0 \rightarrow x = 5$
- $x - 4 = 0 \rightarrow x = 4$

These values, 5 and 4, are the solutions or roots of the polynomial equation.

The FOIL Method

FOIL is an acronym for First, Outside, Inside, Last, and it's a method for multiplying two binomials. It guarantees that all term in the primary binomial is multiplied by any term in the following binomial.

Consider multiplying $(3x + 2)(2x - 5)$ using FOIL:
- **First**: Multiply the first terms of each binomial: $3x * 2x = 6x^2$
- **Outside**: Multiply the outer terms: $3x * (-5) = -15x$
- **Inside**: Multiply the inner terms: $2 * 2x = 4x$
- **Last**: Multiply the last terms: $2 * (-5) = -10$

Combining these results, we get $6x^2 - 15x + 4x - 10$. Simplifying further, the final expression is $6x^2 - 11x - 10$.

Quadratic Expressions
Factoring Quadratic Equations

Factoring quadratic equations is a method to simplify these expressions into a more manageable form. A quadratic equation typically takes the form of $ax^2 + bx + c = 0$. Dividing this into two binomials is the aim.

Consider the quadratic equation $x^2 - 5x + 6 = 0$. In order to factor this, we need to find two values that sum up to -5 (the coefficient of x) and multiply by 6 (the constant term). The numbers -2 and -3 fit this criterion:
- $(x - 2)(x - 3)$

When we expand $(x - 2)(x - 3)$, we get back our original quadratic equation.

Types of Quadratic Equations
1. **Standard Form**: The most common form is $ax^2 + bx + c = 0$, where a, b, and c are constants, and $a \neq 0$.
2. **Factored Form**: This form presents the quadratic as a product of two binomials. For example, $(x - p)(x - q) = 0$, where p and q are the roots of the quadratic equation.
3. **Vertex Form**: $Y = a(x - h)^2 + k$ is the formula for this form, where (h, k) is the vertex of the parabola the quadratic equation forms. This form is useful for graphing and understanding the properties of the parabola.

Equations and Inequalities in ASVAB Mathematics Knowledge
Creating Equations for Word Problems

Word problems require translating a written scenario into a mathematical equation. Here's how to approach them:
1. **Read and Understand**: Carefully read the problem multiple times to understand the scenario.
2. **Identify Key Information**: Highlight or note down the given values and what you need to find. For example, if a problem states a car travels 60 miles in 1.5 hours, note down distance (d = 60 miles) and time (t = 1.5 hours).
3. **Look for Mathematical Operations**: Identify words that indicate specific operations, such as 'sum' for addition or 'product' for multiplication.
4. **Formulate the Equation**: Based on the information and operations, create an equation. Using the car example, you might need to find the speed (s), leading to the equation s = d/t, or s = 60/1.5.

Example Problem: A garden has a length that is twice its width. If the perimeter is 60 feet, what are the garden's dimensions?

Solution: Let the width be x feet. Then, the length is 2x feet. The perimeter (P) is the sum of all sides, so P = 2(length + width) = 2(2x + x) = 60. Simplifying, we get 6x = 60, so x = 10 feet. Therefore, the width is 10 feet, and the length is 20 feet.

Square Roots and Reciprocals

Understanding square roots and reciprocals is crucial for solving various mathematical problems:

1. **Square Roots**: Any number that multiplied by itself yields the original number is said to have the square root. As an example, $5 * 5 = 25$, which is the square root of twenty-five.
2. **Reciprocals**: One divided by a number is the reciprocal of that number. For instance, $1/4$ is the reciprocal of 4.

Example Problem: What is the square root of 144, and what is the reciprocal of the square root?
Solution: The square root of 144 is 12, as $12 * 12 = 144$. The reciprocal of 12 is $1/12$.

Equations with Two Variables

Two-variable equations must be solved for one variable in terms of the other or by identifying particular values that meet the equation's requirements:
1. **Evaluate an Expression with Given Variables**: Substitute the given values into the equation and simplify using the order of operations.
2. **Solve for One Variable in Terms of Another**: To isolate a single variable on a single side, rearrange the equation.

Example Problem: If $x = 4$ and $y = 3$, evaluate the expression $2x + y^2$.
Solution: Substituting the values, we get $2(4) + 3^2 = 8 + 9 = 17$.
Example Problem: Solve for y in terms of x in the equation $2x + 3y = 6$.
Solution: Rearranging, we get $3y = 6 - 2x$, so $y = (6 - 2x)/3$.

Systems of Equations in ASVAB Mathematics Knowledge
Substitution Method

One equation is solved for a single variable using the substitution procedure, and the solution is then entered into the other equation. This approach works especially well when one of the variables in an equation can be solved with ease.
Problem: Solve the system of equations: $y = 2x + 3$ and $3x + 2y = 12$.
Solution:
1. Substitute y from the first equation into the second:
   - The first equation is $y = 2x + 3$.
   - Substitute this expression for y in the second equation, $3x + 2y = 12$.
   - This gives us: $3x + 2(2x + 3) = 12$.
2. Simplify and solve for x:
   - Expand and simplify the equation: $3x + 2(2x + 3) = 12$ becomes $3x + 4x + 6 = 12$.
   - Combine like terms $(3x + 4x)$ to get $7x + 6 = 12$.
   - Subtract 6 from both sides to isolate the term with x: $7x = 12 - 6$, which simplifies to $7x = 6$.
   - To find x, divide both sides by 7: $x = 6/7$.
3. To find y, put x back into the original equation:
   - Now that we know $x = 6/7$, substitute this back into the first equation $(y = 2x + 3)$.
   - Replace x with $6/7$: $y = 2(6/7) + 3$.
   - Simplify the expression: $y = 12/7 + 3$.
   - Convert 3 to a fraction with a denominator of 7 to combine with $12/7$: $3 = 21/7$.
   - Add the fractions: $y = 12/7 + 21/7 = 33/7$.

So, the solution to the system of equations is $x = 6/7$ and $y = 33/7$. This indicates that both of the system's equations are satisfied by these values for x and y.

Solving with Elimination

In order to remove one of the variables and make it simpler to answer for the remaining one, elimination entails adding or subtracting equations.
Example Problem: Solve the system: $2x + y = 7$ and $x - y = 1$.
Solution:

1. Add the two equations: $(2x + y) + (x - y) = 7 + 1$.
2. Simplify: $3x = 8$, $x = 8/3$.
3. Find y by reintroducing x into one of the original equations.

Backsolving

Backsolving is a technique that involves entering the possible answers into the equation and determining which one works. This approach works well for multiple-choice questions.

Example Problem: If $2x - 3 = 5$, what is the value of x?

Solution: Examine every possible solution in the equation until you identify the one that makes sense.

Axis of Symmetry

The notion of the axis of symmetry is important when discussing quadratic equations, which are commonly graphed as parabolas. The parabola is effectively divided into two symmetrical halves by this axis, which is a vertical line. Understanding the symmetry between the two halves is essential to comprehending the characteristics of quadratic functions.

When a, b, and c are constants, a quadratic equation takes the standard form $ax^2 + bx + c$. The formula $x = -b/2a$ can be used to determine the axis of symmetry. With the use of this formula, one can determine the x-coordinate of the parabola, or the place where the axis of symmetry crosses it.

Understanding the Formula x = -b/2a

- The term 'b' in the formula represents the coefficient of the linear term (the term with x) in the quadratic equation.
- The term 'a' is the coefficient of the quadratic term (the term with x^2).
- The x-coordinate of the parabola's vertex can be found using the formula $x = -b/2a$. This x-coordinate is also the equation of the axis of symmetry since the vertex is on the axis of symmetry. For illustration, let's look at the quadratic equation $2x^2 + 8x + 3$.

Example:

Consider the quadratic equation $2x^2 + 8x + 3$. Here, $a = 2$, $b = 8$, and $c = 3$.
1. To find the axis of symmetry, use the formula $x = -b/2a$.
2. Substitute the values of 'b' and 'a': $x = -8/(2*2)$.
3. Simplify the expression: $x = -8/4 = -2$.

Therefore, the axis of symmetry for the quadratic equation $2x^2 + 8x + 3$ is the line $x = -2$. This means that the parabola is symmetric about the vertical line that passes through $x = -2$ on the coordinate plane.

Solving by Factoring

Factoring involves breaking down a polynomial into simpler components. It's useful for solving quadratic equations.

Example Problem: Solve $x^2 - 5x + 6 = 0$ by factoring.

Solution:
1. Factor the quadratic: $(x - 2)(x - 3) = 0$.
2. Set each factor equal to zero: $x - 2 = 0$ or $x - 3 = 0$.
3. Solve for x: $x = 2$ or $x = 3$.

Completing the Square

The completion of squares approach can be used to solve quadratic equations. It is necessary to restructure the equation such that the left side becomes a perfect square trinomial, which has an easy solution.

Example Problem: Solve $x^2 + 6x + 5 = 0$ by completing the square.

Solution:
1. Move the constant term to the right side: $x^2 + 6x = -5$.
2. Find the number that completes the square: $(6/2)^2 = 9$.
3. Add this number to both sides: $x^2 + 6x + 9 = 4$.
4. Rewrite the left side as a squared binomial: $(x + 3)^2 = 4$.

5. Solve for x: $x + 3 = \pm 2$, so $x = -3 \pm 2$, which gives $x = -1$ or $x = -5$.

Roots and Zeros

The values of x that cause a quadratic equation to equal 0 are called its roots or zeros. By solving for x and setting the quadratic equation to zero, they can be found.

Example Problem: Find the roots of $2x^2 - 8x + 6 = 0$.

Solution:

1. Factor the quadratic equation: $2(x - 1)(x - 3) = 0$.
2. Set each factor equal to zero: $x - 1 = 0$ and $x - 3 = 0$.
3. Solve for x: $x = 1$ and $x = 3$.

Discriminants

The area under the square root in the quadratic formula, $b^2 - 4ac$, is the discriminant in a quadratic equation. It establishes what kind of roots the quadratic equation has.

- Two distinct real roots exist if the discriminant is positive.
- There is only one true root if it is zero.
- If negative, there are no real roots, but two complex roots.

Example Problem: Determine the nature of the roots of $x^2 - 4x + 4 = 0$.

Solution:

1. Calculate the discriminant: $(-4)^2 - 4(1)(4) = 0$.
2. The equation has a single real root as the discriminant is zero.

Inequalities

Expressions that have one side that isn't always equal to the other are called inequality. They can be solved similarly to equations, and they can be shown on a number line. Determine the key points and whether the line is solid (inclusive) or dashed (exclusive) to depict an inequality on a number line.

Example Problem: Represent $x > 3$ on a number line.

Solution: Create a number line, mark the number three with a circle, and shade the line to the right of 3.

Solving Inequalities

When attempting to solve an inequality, it is imperative to isolate the variable on one side. When multiplying or dividing by a negative number, the inequality sign must be flipped; otherwise, the procedure is similar to solving equations.

Example Problem: Solve $2x - 5 < 3$.

Solution:

1. Add 5 to both sides: $2x < 8$.
2. Divide by 2: $x < 4$.

Geometry: Basic Terms

One of the basic areas of mathematics that is required for the ASVAB test is geometry. It entails comprehending dimensions, relative positions, forms, and spatial qualities. Proficiency in fundamental geometric concepts is essential for effective problem-solving. Now let's explore a few of these key ideas:

1. **Points**: Points are the most basic units in geometry, akin to atoms in matter. They are employed to delineate angles, lines, and forms. For example, a triangle is defined by three non-collinear points.
2. **Lines**: A line is created by endlessly stretching a thread in both directions. In geometry, it's essential for creating forms and comprehending angles. Lines are the building blocks of many geometric concepts; they can be parallel or intersect.
3. **Line** Segment: A section of a line with two different endpoints is called a line segment. In geometry, it's used to determine distances and create shapes. For example, line segments make up a polygon's sides.
4. **Ray**: Consider a ray as an unlimited laser beam that is directed only in one direction from its source. Angle measurements and geometric constructions both use it. Angle definition is fundamentally based on rays.
5. **Midpoint**: Similar to a line segment's balance point is the midpoint. It's employed for creating symmetrical

forms and splitting line segments. In order to divide a form or line segment into equal parts, you must first find its midpoint.

6. **Bisector**: An object is divided into two equal halves by a bisector. It could be a segment bisecting another segment or a line bisecting an angle. In order to construct symmetrical forms and validate geometric theorems, bisectors are essential.

7. **Collinear Points**: Collinear points are like pearls on a string, lying in a straight line. They are important in understanding linearity in geometry and are used in proving geometric properties related to lines.

8. **Plane**: Comparable to an endlessly long flat sheet in all directions is a plane. The majority of geometric shapes are found on this two-dimensional surface. It is essential to comprehend planes in order to solve and visualize two-dimensional problems.

9. **Coplanar**: Similar to drawings on paper, coplanar points or lines occur on the same plane. Understanding coplanar elements is crucial for resolving issues with angles and forms in shared spaces.

10. **Perpendicular Lines**: Right angles between perpendicular lines create a 'L' shape. They are essential for building rectangles and squares as well as comprehending correct angles. A fundamental idea in many geometric arguments is **perpendicularity.**

11. **Parallel** Lines: Like train tracks, parallel lines never meet, no matter how far they are apart. They are crucial for comprehending geometric forms like parallelograms and for resolving issues with angles created by crossing lines.

12. **Slope**: A line's slope reveals its direction and degree of steepness. It is comparable to calculating a hill's incline. Since slope is a fundamental idea in coordinate geometry and is utilized in equations involving lines, it is essential for resolving a wide range of algebraic and geometric issues.

Types of Angles

1. **Right Angle**: A right angle is similar to the corner of a square or rectangle because it is exactly ninety degrees. It is a fundamental angle in geometry, and the vertex is typically indicated by a little square.

2. **Acute Angle**: Less than ninety degrees is an acute angle. It resembles a thin, pointy wedge. Many geometric shapes, particularly triangles, have acute angles.

3. **Obtuse Angle**: More than 90 degrees but less than 180 degrees is considered an obtuse angle. It resembles an open, wide wedge. Obtuse triangles frequently have obtuse angles.

4. **Straight Angle**: A straight angle, which looks like a straight line, is precisely 180 degrees. In essence, it splits the plane in half.

5. **Full Angle**: A full circle is represented by an angle that is 360 degrees in length. It is the entire arc surrounding a point.

6. **Angle Bisector**: An angle is divided into two equal pieces by an angle bisector. It is a ray or line that precisely halves an angle to produce two congruent angles.

Pairs of Angles

1. **Complementary Angles**: When two angles sum up to ninety degrees, they are in harmony. They might be nearby or they might not. For instance, a 30 degree angle has a 60 degree complement.

2. **Supplementary Angles**: If the sum of two angles is 180 degrees, then they are supplementary. They can be either neighboring or non-adjacent, much like complimentary angles. A typical illustration would be a pair of linear angles.

3. **Vertical Angles**: Two lines that cross one another create two sets of vertical, or opposing, angles. These angles are equal in measure and always congruent.

4. **Adjacent Angles**: Although they do not overlap, adjacent angles have a same vertex and side. They are adjacent to one another. Every corner of a rectangle has two sets of neighboring angles.

5. **Linear Pair**: When two lines intersect, two neighboring angles are created, known as a linear pair. A linear pair's angles are always supplementary.

6. **Corresponding Angles**: The angles in matching corners are referred to as corresponding angles when two lines are intersected by a single line, also known as the transversal. Corresponding angles in parallel lines that a transversal cuts are equivalent.

7. **Congruent Angles**: Congruent angles might be in multiple orientations or positions, but they always have the same angle measure. They frequently occur in related geometric shapes.

Polygons: The Building Blocks of Geometry
Defining Polygons
A polygon is a geometric shape that has a closed route formed around it by straight lines. The intersections of these lines are called vertices, and they are referred to as sides. Triangles (three sides), quadrilaterals (four sides), pentagons (five sides), hexagons (six sides), and so on are some examples. All of the sides and angles of a regular polygon are equal. They have equal angles on both sides, making them equiangular.

Angles in Polygons
- **Interior Angles**: These are the polygon's interior angles. For example, in a pentagon, an internal angle is formed at each corner when two sides converge.
- **Exterior Angles**: Produced by expanding one of the polygon's sides. Extending a side of a hexagon creates an external angle next to an interior angle.
- **Calculating Angles**: The sum of interior angles in a polygon is given by the formula $S = (n - 2) \times 180°$, where n is the number of sides.

Apothems
A line drawn perpendicular to one of the sides of a regular polygon from its center is called an apothem. It is essential for figuring out how big regular polygons are.

Triangles: The Simplest Polygons
Parts of a Triangle
- **Altitude**: A line from a vertex perpendicular to the opposite side.
- **Base**: The side of the triangle considered as the 'bottom'.
- **Vertex**: The corner where two sides meet.
- **Median**: A path that runs from a vertex to the other side's midway.
- **Centroid**: The intersection of every median.

Types of Triangles
By Sides: Isosceles (two equal sides), Equilateral (all sides equal), Scalene (no equal sides).
By Angles: Acute (all angles $< 90°$), Right (one $90°$ angle), Obtuse (one angle $> 90°$).

Quadrilaterals: Four-Sided Figures
Types of Quadrilaterals
- **Parallelogram**: The opposing sides are equal and parallel.
- **Rectangle**: Two parallelograms joined at their angles.
- **Rhombus**: Every side of a parallelogram being equal.
- **Square**: A rectangular shape with equal sides.
- **Trapezoid**: Just a single set of parallel sides.

Circles: The Round Geometry
Parts of a Circle
- **Radius**: A line drawn between the perimeter and the center.
- **Diameter**: A line that passes across the middle and touches two circumferential points.
- **Chord**: A line segment within the circle, touching the circumference at two points.
- **Tangent**: A line that makes exactly one point contact with the circle.

Angles and Arcs in Circles
- **Central Angle**: An angle created by two radii is called the central angle of a circle. The circle's center is where this angle's vertex is located. The angle formed by the meeting point of two lines drawn from a circle's center to

its edge, for instance, is known as the central angle.

- **Inscribed Angle**: Two chords in a circle that intersect at a single point on the circle's circumference constitute an inscribed angle. Unlike the central angle, the vertex of an inscribed angle is on the circle itself. An inscribed angle's measure is always half that of the arc it intersects. An inscribed angle, for example, will measure 60° if it intercepts a 120° angle.
- **Arc**: A section of a circle's circumference is called an arc. It is the portion of the circle's edge that is curled. Arcs can be categorized as major or minor according on their size. Any arc that is less than half the circle's radius and less than 180° is considered a minor arc. It is the smaller curve on a circle that is between two points. On the other hand, a major arc is larger than 180° and makes up more than half of the circle's circumference. On a circle, it is the bigger curve that connects two points. If you are aware of the circle's radius and center angle, you can compute the length of an arc. An arc representing a 90° central angle, for instance, would make up a fourth of the circumference of a circle with a radius of 10 cm.

Solid Geometry
Rectangular Solid
A three-dimensional structure with six faces that are all rectangle-shaped is called a rectangular solid, sometimes referred to as a rectangular prism. Its dimensions are height, breadth, and length.

- **Surface Area Calculation**: The sum of the areas of a rectangular solid's six faces yields the solid's surface area. A solid's surface area is equal to $2lw + 2lh + 2wh$ when its dimensions are length (l), width (w), and height (h).
- **Practical Example**: If a box has a length of 8 cm, a width of 5 cm, and a height of 3 cm, its surface area is $2(8 \times 5) + 2(8 \times 3) + 2(5 \times 3) = 142$ cm².

Cylinder
A solid geometric shape with two parallel circular bases joined by a curved surface is called a cylinder. Its height and radius define it.

- **Surface Area**: The combined regions of a cylinder's two bases and curving surface make up its surface area. The formula is $2\pi r^2 + 2\pi rh$, where (r) stands for radius and (h) for height.
- **Example**: The surface area of a cylinder with a height of 10 cm and a radius of 4 cm is equal to $2\pi(4^2) + 2\pi(4 \times 10) = 351.68$ cm² (using pi ≈ 3.14).

Coordinate Geometry
Coordinate Grid
A two-dimensional plane divided by a vertical (y-axis) and horizontal (x-axis) line is called a coordinate grid. The coordinates of each point (x, y) on this grid are used to identify it.

Use: Equations and inequalities are graphically represented by plotting points, lines, and curves.

Slope
In a coordinate grid, a line's slope indicates both its direction and steepness. It is computed as the ratio of the horizontal (x) to vertical (y) change, and is commonly stated as "rise over run."

- **Slope Formula**: $m = \{\text{Delta } y\} / \{\text{Delta } x\}$ or $m = \{y_2 - y_1\} / \{x_2 - x_1\}$.
- **Example**: If you have two points (1, 2) and (3, 6), the slope of the line through these points is $\{6 - 2\} / \{3 - 1\} = 2$.

GENERAL SCIENCE

The ASVAB's General Science component assesses your comprehension of a wide range of scientific topics in-depth. This chapter attempts to break down each important topic and give a comprehensive summary to guarantee a well-rounded exam preparation. This area requires a balanced understanding of several scientific principles, ranging from the physical sciences to the life sciences.

Life Science: The Foundation of Biological Understanding

- **Health and Nutrition**: This is an important area of life science that involves knowing how nutrients function in the human body. It includes macronutrients such as proteins, lipids, and carbs; each has a specific purpose, ranging from supplying energy to repairing cells. Carbohydrates provide the bulk of energy and are converted into glucose, whilst lipids store energy and aid in the production of hormones. Amino acid-based proteins are essential for the development and maintenance of cells.
- **Micronutrients**: For the body to function at its best, certain vitamins and minerals are necessary in little amounts. A, D, E, and K are fat-soluble vitamins; the B vitamin group is water-soluble, and each group of vitamins has a specific function in cellular functions. Numerous biological functions rely on minerals such as sodium, potassium, magnesium, and calcium.
- **Other Essential Substances**: Water, which makes up a large amount of body weight, is essential to every cellular process. Despite being indigestible, fiber is essential for preserving intestinal health.
- **Nutrition-Related Diseases**: Unbalances in micro and macronutrients can lead to diseases like scurvy, diabetes, hypertension, and iron deficiency anemia.

The Human Body: A Complex System

The study of the body's components and the numerous mechanisms that keep it running is the broad and complex discipline of human anatomy. A fundamental understanding of the functions and relationships of the body's systems is necessary to pass the ASVAB. Comprehending the interplay between these systems is essential to understanding the basic principles of human biology.

Skeleton and Muscles: The Framework of Movement

- **Skeletal System**: The skeletal system, which is made up of bones and cartilage, gives the body's organs structural support and defense. Together, the flexible collagen substance known as cartilage and the hard phosphate bones allow the bone marrow to move and create blood.
- **Muscular System**: This system, which consists of smooth, skeletal, and cardiac muscles, collaborates with the skeletal system to provide movement. Every type of muscle has a distinct function; smooth muscles support organ functions, skeletal muscles enable movement, and cardiac muscles control heartbeats.

Respiration: The Essence of Life

One vital biological process that involves exchanging gases necessary to sustain life is respiration. It's a sophisticated system that includes a number of bodily organs and structures, each of which has a distinct function in maintaining effective gas exchange. This section explores the mechanics of respiration in greater detail, emphasizing the important elements and how they work.

1. **Inhalation and Exhalation**: The body uses respiration primarily to take in oxygen and release carbon dioxide. Drawing air into the lungs during inhalation allows oxygen to be taken up by the blood. The process of exhaling involves expelling carbon dioxide, a waste product of cellular metabolism, and air from the lungs.
2. **The Role of the Lungs**: The respiratory system's main organ is the lung. These are the spongy organs filled with air that are situated on the two sides of the chest, or thorax. The main job of the lungs is to enable gas exchange, which is the process by which blood absorbs oxygen from the atmosphere and releases carbon dioxide into the atmosphere. Each lung has two lobes on the left and three on the right.
3. **Trachea and Bronchi**: The tube that joins the neck (pharynx) to the lungs is called the trachea, or windpipe. It divides into two major bronchi, each of which goes to a single lung. Within the lungs, these bronchi further split into smaller branches known as bronchioles. Air travels through the trachea and bronchi, making sure it enters the lungs deeply.
4. **Alveoli and Gas Exchange**: Little air sacs known as alveoli are found at the end of bronchioles. These are where gas exchange takes place. An extensive network of capillaries envelops alveoli. The blood in the capillaries receives oxygen from the inhaled air through the thin walls of the alveoli. The blood's carbon dioxide is simultaneously transported to the alveoli for exhalation.
5. **Breathing Mechanism**: The diaphragm and intercostal muscles regulate breathing. Beneath the lungs lies a muscle dome called the diaphragm. During inhalation, the diaphragm flattens and contracts, creating a vacuum that drives airflow into the lungs. The intercostal muscles between the ribs also aid in extending. The

diaphragm relaxes and takes on its typical dome form during exhalation, forcing air out of the lungs.

6. **Oxygen Transport**: Red blood cells transport oxygen to the body's cells after it enters the circulation. Oxygen is transported inside the organism by the protein termed hemoglobin, which is present in red blood cells. This oxygen is used by cells for a variety of metabolic functions, which releases energy.

7. **Carbon Dioxide Removal**: The bloodstream returns carbon dioxide, a consequence of cellular respiration, to the lungs. At the time of exhale, it is then released from the body.

Blood and Circulation: The Lifeline of the Body

The heart, blood vessels, and blood itself are all part of the complex network that is the circulatory system, which is essential to the body's homeostasis and general health. The intricacy and effectiveness of this system are vital to life support because they enable the movement of necessary materials throughout the body. Let's examine the key components and their functions in more detail.

- **The Heart's Role**: The heart, a muscular organ located in the chest, serves as the primary pump of the circulatory system. Its four chambers are composed of two ventricles (bottom chambers) and two atria (top chambers). Blood that has lost oxygen is pumped from the body to the lungs by the right side of the heart. Blood that is high in oxygen is drawn from the lungs by the left side and circulated throughout the body. This dual-pump system provides an uninterrupted flow of oxygenated blood to the body's tissues and organs.

- **Blood Vessels**: Different kinds of blood arteries make up the circulatory system:
  1. **Arteries**: From the heart, these vessels transport oxygenated blood to the body's tissues. The aorta, the main artery, splits into smaller arteries, which then split into arterioles and, at last, capillaries.
  2. **Veins**: Deoxygenated blood is returned to the heart through veins. They are equipped with valves that guarantee blood flows only in the upward flow of the heart and prevent it from flowing in the opposite way.
  3. **Capillaries**: The exchange of nutrients, waste materials, oxygen, and carbon dioxide between the blood and the body's cells takes place in these tiniest blood arteries.

- **Blood Components and Functions**:
  1. **Red Blood Cells (Erythrocytes)**: Hemoglobin, a protein found in these cells, binds oxygen and carries it from the lungs to the body's tissues. They also return waste products like carbon dioxide to the lungs.
  2. **White Blood Cells (Leukocytes)**: Comprising an essential component of the immune system, these cells shield the body from external threats and pathogens.
  3. **Plasma**: This fluid portion of blood is made up of proteins, ions, and water. It acts as a conduit for waste materials, hormones, and nutrients.
  4. **Platelets (Thrombocytes)**: The parts of broken down cells are necessary for blood clotting and healing of wounds.

- **Cardiovascular Health and Diseases**: For general health, the circulatory system must be in good working order. Heart failure, coronary artery disease, and hypertension are common cardiovascular disorders that are characterized by high blood pressure and blockage of the coronary arteries. Because of the potential for major consequences, these disorders highlight how crucial it is to maintain cardiovascular health through a balanced diet, consistent exercise, and abstaining from risk factors like smoking and binge drinking.

- **Blood Pressure and Circulation**: Blood pressure is the force that blood flowing through a blood artery applies to its walls. It is a vital sign of the health of the circulatory system. Heart attacks, strokes, and other issues can result from high blood pressure's damaging effects on blood vessels and straining the heart.

Blood Types: The Classification of Blood

Red blood cells' Rhesus (Rh) factor and the presence of particular antigens are used to classify blood types. Depending on the Rh factor, the four primary blood types (A, B, AB, and O) are further divided into positive and negative categories. Understanding immunological reactions and using blood transfusions depend on this classification.

- **Antigens and Rh Factor**: Blood type is determined by antigens, and the Rh factor shows whether a certain protein is present on red blood cells.

- **Universal Donor and Recipient**: Because of their similar antigen profiles, blood types O and AB are regarded as the universal donor and receiver, respectively.

Digestion and Excretion: The Essentials of Nutrient Processing and Waste Management

The human body's intricate network of organs and functions allows it to remove waste and obtain nutrients from meals, which is a marvel of biological engineering. This section examines the digestive and excretory systems, highlighting their roles and relevance.

- **The Digestive Journey**: Food enters the mouth and starts the process of digestion. Saliva's abundance of enzymes starts the food's breakdown process. Food is chewed into a bolus, or manageable mass, which is subsequently swallowed. Peristalsis, a rhythmic constriction of the esophagus, forces the bolus into the stomach. Here, the food is further broken down by stomach acids and enzymes, becoming chyme, a semi-liquid material.
- **Small Intestine's Role**: The small intestine, a lengthy, coiled tube where the majority of nutrient absorption takes place, receives the chyme after that. The lining of the small intestine, which is coated in microscopic projections known as villi, increases surface area to facilitate effective absorption of nutrients.
- **Large Intestine and Waste Formation**: The large intestine receive the leftover undigested material. This is where waste material is compressed into feces and water and certain nutrients are absorbed. The excrement is then retained in the rectum until the anus opens to discharge it.
- **Excretory System**: In tandem with digestion, the excretory system is essential for preserving the interior environment of the body. It consists of the bladder, ureter, urethra, lungs, and skin. Urine is produced when the kidneys filter blood, eliminating waste and extra chemicals. The lungs release carbon dioxide as a result of cellular respiration. Sweating allows the skin to expel waste and maintain body temperature.
- **Digestive Enzymes and Acids**:
  1. **Salivary Amylase**: This enzyme in saliva kickstarts the digestion of carbohydrates.
  2. **Gastric Acids**: These acids in the stomach aid in protein digestion and activate various digestive enzymes.
  3. **Pepsin**: An enzyme in the stomach that reduces proteins to smaller peptides.
- **Liver and Pancreas**: The pancreas secretes enzymes like lipase and amylase, which are essential for breaking down fats and carbohydrates, while the liver produces bile, which aids in the digestion of fats.
- **Bile**: Bile, which is made by the liver and kept in the gallbladder, is used in the breakdown of fat and the elimination of waste.

The Nervous System: The Body's Communication Network

The nervous system is the main communication and control system of the body. It consists of a vast network of neurons, the spinal cord, and the brain.

1. **Brain Functionality**: The nervous system's command center, the brain, interprets sensory data and determines how to respond. It has two hemispheres and three main sections: the brainstem, which regulates involuntary movements like breathing, the cerebellum, which coordinates movement and balance, and the cerebrum, which is in charge of higher cognitive functions.
2. **Neurons**: These are the basic parts of the nervous system that distribute messages throughout the body. In order to facilitate communication, each neuron has an extension that connects to another neuron and a nucleus.
3. **Spinal Cord**: The primary informational channel between the brain and peripheral nerve system is this one. Information about sensation and movement is transmitted while it is shielded by the vertebrae.
4. **Central and Peripheral Nervous Systems**: The brain and spinal cord make up the central nervous system, whereas all the nerves that are not part of the central nervous system are part of the peripheral nervous system. It is separated into the autonomic (which regulates involuntary functions) and somatic (which controls voluntary motions) nervous systems.

Reproduction: The Continuity of Life

The process through which creatures create offspring is called reproduction, and it is essential to the survival of species. There are two primary varieties of it: asexual and sexual.

1. **Asexual Reproduction**: This is the reproduction of a single organism without the genetic contribution of another. It includes processes like mitosis, which is the separation of one cell into two cells with identical genes.
2. **Sexual Reproduction in Humans**: Involves the joining of a male gamete (sperm) and a female gamete (egg) to create a zygote. The zygote develops into a new individual through cell division.

3. **Meiosis**: A specific type of cell division that ensures genetic variety by resulting in gametes with half as many chromosomes.
4. **Menstrual Cycle and Ovulation**: The female menstrual cycle, which begins with ovulation—the release of an egg from the ovary—readies the body for possible pregnancy.
5. **Fertilization and Embryonic Development**: When a sperm cell successfully fuses with an egg, a zygote is created, which is known as fertilization. After implanting in the uterus, this zygote initiates the process of embryonic development.
6. **Blood Types and Immunology**: Based on the presence of particular antigens on red blood cells, blood types are categorized. Blood is further classified as positive or negative by the Rh factor. It is essential to comprehend blood types in order to administer safe blood transfusions and to comprehend immunological responses.

Human Pathogens: Agents of Disease

Pathogens are microorganisms or particulates that can infect people and cause illness. They consist of fungus, viruses, and bacteria.
1. **Bacteria**: These prokaryotic, single-celled organisms may be advantageous to people or detrimental to them.
2. **Viruses**: organisms that are not alive but can infect cells and cause illness.
3. **Vaccination and Immunization**: These are techniques to develop immunity against particular pathogens, offering defense against a range of infectious illnesses.

Exploring the Intricacies of Genetics

The intriguing field of genetics explores genes and their function in variation and heredity in living things. The essential ideas of genetics, including DNA structure and genetic heredity, will be covered in this thorough investigation.
1. **Genes and Genetic Makeup**: The fundamental building blocks of heredity, genes, are DNA sequences that determine particular features. The genotype, or whole genetic composition, of an organism is made up of distinct alleles, or variations on a single gene. The visible physical or biochemical traits of an organism, on the other hand, are known as its phenotype and are influenced by both its genotype and its surroundings.
2. **Dominant and Recessive Traits**: In genetics, traits are frequently classified as dominant or recessive. Recessive qualities need the presence of two recessive alleles in order to manifest, whereas dominant features can manifest with just one dominant allele.
3. **DNA**: The complex molecule known as deoxyribonucleic acid (DNA) is home to the genetic instructions necessary for all known living things to develop, function, grow, and reproduce. Adenine, guanine, thymine, and cytosine are among the nucleotides that make up DNA, and they are arranged in a double helix form.
4. **Cell Division - Meiosis and Mitosis**: Meiosis and mitosis are the two main processes that lead to cell replication. Genetic diversity is produced during the meiotic process, which creates gametes by combining the genetic material of two different people. Somatic (non-sex) cells divide into two daughter cells that share the same genetic makeup as the parent cell throughout the mitotic process.
5. **Chromosomal Basis of Inheritance**: There are 23 pairs of chromosomes in humans; chromosomes are lengthy DNA molecules that contain genes. One pair of sex chromosomes, designated as XX for girls and XY for men, is included among these chromosomes and determines the individual's biological sex.
6. **Punnett Squares and Genetic Predictions**: A Punnett square diagram is a tool for genotype prediction from parental alleles in offspring. It uses a grid with boxes representing potential offspring genotypes based on the pairing of alleles from each parent.
7. **Key Figures and Terms in Genetics**:
   - **Gregor Mendel**: Mendel, who is frequently called the "Father of Genetics," developed the theory of genetic inheritance through his studies with pea plants.
   - **Gametes**: These are the reproductive cells, which contain half of an organism's haploid genetic information (eggs in females and sperm in men).
   - **Diploid and Haploid**: Whereas haploid cells, such as gametes, only have one set of chromosomes, diploid cells have two complete sets—one from each parent.
   - **Genetic Code**: the arrangement of nucleotides in DNA that contains the instructions needed to build proteins, which are essential for carrying out various biological processes.

- **Nucleotides**: the fundamental units of DNA and RNA, which are composed of a nitrogenous base (adenine, thymine, cytosine, guanine, and uracil in RNA), a sugar, and a phosphate group.
- **Double Helix**: DNA's twisted ladder structure, which is made up of two strands of linked nucleotides.

The World of Cells and Ecology

The two main categories of life's smallest units are prokaryotic and eukaryotic cells. Bacteria are examples of prokaryotic cells, which are devoid of membrane-bound organelles and a clearly identifiable nucleus. Their DNA is free to move around the cytoplasm. Eukaryotic cells, which are found in creatures such as humans, have different organelles and a clearly defined nucleus. These cells may be found in multicellular organisms or as single cells.

Unlike prokaryotic cells, where DNA is distributed throughout the cytoplasm, eukaryotic cells contain genetic material within their nucleus. Prokaryotes reproduce by binary fission, whereas eukaryotes multiply by means of meiosis and mitosis.

Plant cells have a different composition of organelles than do animal cells. The majority of plant cells lack lysosomes, which are organelles that house chloroplasts for photosynthesis, plastids, and cell walls. The nucleus, cell membrane, Golgi apparatus, ribosomes, mitochondria, endoplasmic reticulum, cytoplasm, and vacuoles are shared by both cell types.

Respiration and Cellular Functions

Numerous biological processes, like the synthesis of energy in mitochondria and the formation and removal of trash by lysosomes, are mirrored in cells. They use vacuoles to control internal fluids and cell walls or membranes to keep them isolated from the outside world.

Glucose is converted by cellular respiration into ATP, the body's energy currency. The first phase of the procedure, called glycolysis, turns glucose into pyruvate, NADH, and ATP. Acetyl CoA is created when pyruvate is oxidized, starting the Citric Acid Cycle and generating CO_2, ATP, $FADH_2$, and NADH.

Cell Division: Mitosis and Meiosis

In somatic cells, the process of mitosis, which includes prophase, metaphase, anaphase, and telophase, produces two identical daughter cells. Meiosis in gametes, on the other hand, results in four genetically distinct cells, each having half as many chromosomes as the parent cell.

Ecology: The Study of Organisms and Their Environment

Ecology is a research field of living things and their interactions with their environment, ranging from microscopic organisms to massive mammals. It is essential to comprehend fundamental ecological systems, processes, and the effects of changing environmental conditions.

Key Ecological Concepts

- **Biosphere**: All life on Earth is included in the biosphere, which emphasizes how interrelated all living things are with their environments.
- **Biome**: A biome is an assemblage of habitats that generate unique ecological communities and share comparable climates and creatures.
- **Ecosystem**: Living and nonliving elements interacting in a particular context make up an ecosystem.
- **Community**: A community represents the relationships between various groups in a particular location.
- **Population**: All the animals that live together and are part of a particular species in a specific region are considered members of the population.

Ecological Classifications

- **Producers**: organisms with the ability to produce their own sustenance, usually by photosynthesis.
- **Decomposers**: organisms that recycle nutrients back into the ecosystem by decomposing dead organic stuff.
- **Scavengers**: Creatures that consume dead organisms.
- **Consumers**: Organisms that get their nourishment and energy from other organisms.
- **Consumer Hierarchy**: This comprises omnivores as tertiary consumers, carnivores as secondary consumers, and herbivores as main consumers.

Food Webs and Energy Flow

Food webs show how creatures in an ecosystem interact with one another and exchange energy. They show how the delicate balance of nature is maintained by showing who eats whom.

Classification of Living Things

The following hierarchical categories are used to classify living things: domain, kingdom, phylum, class, order, family, genus, and species. The taxonomy system aids in comprehending the traits and evolutionary links of various creatures.

Domains of Life

- **Eukaryota**: This domain comprises various kingdoms, which are distinguished by having nucleated cells, such as plants, animals, and fungi.
- **Bacteria and Archaea**: Prokaryotic organisms are found in these domains and are characterized by the absence of membrane-bound organelles and a nucleus.

Exploring Earth and Space Science

From the minute intricacies of geology to the broad ideas of meteorology and atmospheric science, a wide range of subjects are covered in the study of Earth and space science. The purpose of this part is to give a thorough review of these topics, which are necessary for comprehending our planet and its place in the cosmos.

Geology: The Earth's Story

Understanding both large-scale occurrences like seismic activity and mountain formation as well as smaller-scale processes like mineral formation is the goal of geology, the science of the Earth. It is essential to have a fundamental understanding of the various geological formations, including plains, mountains, plateaus, and canyons.

The composition of the Earth is a marvel of layers, with the semi-solid mantle sitting on top of the liquid metal outer core, which is surrounded by a solid sphere of iron and nickel. The crust, which contains the continents and seas, is situated above these layers. Comprehending these strata facilitates an understanding of seismic activity and continental drift.

The Earth's lithosphere, that includes the crust and upper mantle, is divided by tectonic plates. Earthquakes and volcanic eruptions are caused by the movement and interaction of these plates, which are propelled by subsurface forces. The progressive movement of continents from a single landmass, Pangea, to their current positions is explained by the idea of continental drift.

Rocks and Their Formation

Three main types of rocks make up the Earth's crust, which is a rich tapestry of geological history: igneous, sedimentary, and metamorphic. Every kind narrates a different tale of the processes that have shaped Earth's past and present.

- **Igneous Rocks**: These rocks originate from the Earth's ferocious depths. They are created when lava, or molten rock that has erupted onto the surface of the Earth, cools and solidifies. Igneous rocks can be divided into two distinct categories according to where they solidified. Large, visible crystals occur when intrusive igneous rocks, like granite, cool gradually beneath the Earth's surface. Basalt and other extrusive igneous rocks cool rapidly on the surface of the Earth, leaving behind little or no visible crystals and fine-grained textures.
- **Sedimentary Rocks**: Similar to time capsules, sedimentary rocks hold information about the Earth's surface conditions spanning millions of years. They originate from the buildup and compacting of sediments, which may contain organic material, mineral grains, and pieces of other rocks. These sediments become compacted and cemented together over time. Common examples are limestone, which is frequently made up of accumulated coral fragments or the shells of marine animals, and sandstone, which is made up of particles the size of sand. Fossils are found in sedimentary rocks frequently and provide important hints about former habitats and life.
- **Metamorphic Rocks**: Rocks classified as metamorphic have undergone a significant alteration. They come from previously existing igneous, sedimentary, or even other metamorphic rocks that are found deep beneath the Earth's crust and undergo metamorphosis under intense pressure and temperature. Without melting them, this technique modifies the structure and chemistry of the minerals. For example, shale makes slate, whereas limestone forms marble. These rocks undergo such drastic alterations that they might no longer resemble their initial shape, offering insights into the dynamic processes taking place within the Earth.

All things considered, these three kinds of rocks are not only essential elements of the planet's crust but also important markers of geological processes and the planet's evolutionary past. Deciphering them is essential to solving the enigmas surrounding the origin and eons-long changes of our planet.

The Earth's Cycles

The preservation of the Earth's temperature, weather patterns, and life itself depend heavily on its complex and interwoven cycles. The rock, water, carbon, nitrogen, and air cycles are among them; each one contributes differently to the biological equilibrium of the earth.

- **Atmospheric Cycle**: The movement of air masses and the global exchange of heat and moisture are both components of the atmospheric cycle. The Earth's climate and weather patterns are largely controlled by this cycle. It involves intricate interactions between the atmosphere and the Earth's surface that are impacted by human activity, geographic features, and solar radiation.
- **Carbon Cycle**: The environment recycles carbon dioxide through a number of mechanisms known as the "carbon cycle." This cycle consists of respiration, which releases carbon dioxide back into the atmosphere, and photosynthesis, which allows plants to take carbon dioxide and release oxygen. In addition to being necessary for life on Earth, the carbon cycle is a major factor in climate change since fluctuations in carbon dioxide levels can impact worldwide temperatures.
- **Nitrogen Cycle**: The nitrogen cycle is the process by which nitrogen undergoes various chemical transformations as it passes through ecosystems on land, in the atmosphere, and in the water. This cycle consists of three stages: nitrogen fixation, nitrification, and denitrification. Since nitrogen is an essential component of amino acids and nucleic acids, it is required for all living organisms.
- **Rock Cycle**: The changing of rocks through different geological processes is referred to as the "rock cycle," which is an ongoing process. As previously mentioned, this cycle involves the creation of igneous, sedimentary, and metamorphic rocks and is fueled by surface processes such as weathering and erosion as well as interior heat from the Earth.
- **Water Cycle**: The constant flow of water across, above, and below the Earth's surface is known as the water cycle. Runoff, precipitation, condensation, and evaporation are all parts of this cycle. Heat must be transferred throughout the planet by the water cycle, which is an essential component of the Earth's climate system.
- **Meteorology**: Understanding and forecasting weather patterns requires a solid understanding of meteorology, the study of the Earth's atmosphere. Meteorologists examine air temperature, pressure, wind speed, humidity, and other atmospheric parameters using a variety of instruments and models. Their efforts are essential for weather forecasting, which has a big impact on transportation, agriculture, and disaster preparedness.
- **Earth's Atmospheric Layers**: There are five different layers that make up the Earth's atmosphere, and each has a unique set of properties and function within the climate system:
  1. **Troposphere**: the lowest layer, which is also the location of most atmospheric water vapor and where meteorological events occur.
  2. **Stratosphere**: Includes the ozone layer, which disperses and absorbs UV rays from the sun.
  3. **Mesosphere**: the middle layer, where meteors burn when they enter Earth's atmosphere and where temperatures drop with height.
  4. **Thermosphere**: Here, where the auroras are found, is a layer of air that rapidly warms with altitude.
  5. **Exosphere**: the outermost layer, extending into space as the atmosphere thins.
- **Weather Fronts and Clouds**: Predicting weather conditions requires an understanding of weather fronts and cloud types:
  1. **Weather Fronts**: These represent the limits separating several air masses. When two air masses collide but remain motionless, it forms a stationary front. When a colder air mass pushes aside a warmer one, a cold front forms, which frequently results in bright sky. When a warm air mass passes over a cold one, it forms a warm front, which usually brings with it heavy precipitation.
  2. **Cloud Types**: The appearance and height of clouds are used for categorized them. Stratus clouds are low-lying that frequently herald rain. Fair weather is typically indicated by fluffy, mid-level cumulus clouds. Cirrus clouds are ice crystal-based, high-altitude clouds that frequently herald a change in the weather.

To put it briefly, these cycles and atmospheric occurrences are essential to comprehending Earth's ecosystem and forecasting changes in the weather and climate. They affect every facet of life on Earth and are interrelated.

Understanding Our Solar System

With the Sun as its center, a giant star whose gravitational pull controls the motion of planets and other celestial bodies, our Solar structure is a dynamic and intricate structure. It consists of eight planets, all of which have distinct features and habitats that are influenced by how close they are to the Sun.

- **Planetary Order**: The planets are Mercury, Venus, Earth, Mars, Jupiter, Saturn, Uranus, and Neptune, starting with the Sun. The distances at which each planet orbits the Sun have an impact on their surface temperatures, atmospheric compositions, and capacity to support life.
- **Celestial Bodies**: Our Solar System is made up of planets and their orbiting moons, comets made of ice and dust, meteoroids, and asteroids, most of which are located in the asteroid belt between Mars and Jupiter. The remains of meteors hitting the ground are called meteorites. Meteors are meteoroids which flare up when they reached the atmosphere of the planet.
- **The Kuiper Belt**: The Kuiper Belt, which contains frozen rocks and dwarf planets like Pluto—once thought to be the ninth planet in our solar system—lies beyond Neptune.

Effects of Earth's Position in Space

The orientation and position of Earth in space have a big impact on the natural phenomena that occur there.

- **Seasons**: The Earth's orbit around the Sun and its axial tilt are what cause the seasons. Seasonal variations result from the Earth's rotation around the Sun, which distributes sunlight throughout the planet's surface.
- **Lunar Eclipse**: When the Earth passes in front of the Sun and a full moon, a lunar eclipse happens, shadowing the moon. Because of this arrangement, the Moon is frequently given a reddish tint as the Sun's rays cannot reach it directly.
- **Solar Eclipse**: A solar eclipse is a natural occurrence that occurs when the Moon moves in front of the Sun, causing a shadow to be thrown across the planet. This unusual occurrence momentarily blocks out the Sun's light, producing a striking spectacle that may be seen from some places on Earth.

Physical science

Physical science is a vast field that covers components of chemistry and physics and studies non-living entities. Understanding it is crucial to understanding how the entire universe functions, from the smallest particles to the largest structures.

Measurement in Science

In physical science, measurement is essential because it enables the quantification and comparison of many events. Common units of measurement include force (newtons), electrical charge (coulombs), weight (kilograms), time (seconds), and distance (meters). In measuring, consistency in measurements is referred to as precision, and the degree of accuracy in a measurement denotes its proximity to the true value.

Fundamentals of Physics

The study of the nature and characteristics of matter and energy is known as physics. It includes a wide range of topics, from the extremely small (subatomic particles) to the very large (cosmic phenomena).

- **Mass and Weight**: No matter where an object is, its mass, or amount of matter, remains constant. But weight—which varies based on an object's location in the universe—is the force that gravity applies to an object's mass.
- **Motion**: The study of object motion in space and time is included in this. Three key ideas are acceleration (change in velocity), velocity (speed with direction), and speed. The amount that an object's position has changed is measured by a vector quantity called displacement.
- **Energy**: The ability to perform tasks is known as energy, and it can be either potential (stored energy) or kinetic (energy of motion). Energy can only be changed from one form to another; it cannot be created or destroyed, according to the rule of conservation of energy.
- **Forces**: Objects move or alter their motion due to forces. The four fundamental forces are gravity, strong nuclear force, weak nuclear force, and electromagnetic force. The framework provided by Newton's laws of motion

allows one to comprehend how forces impact an object's motion.

Newton's Laws of Motion

- **First Law (Law of Inertia)**: Until an imbalanced force acts upon an object, it remains at rest or continues in motion in the same direction and at the same pace.
- **Second Law**: An object's acceleration is inversely related to its mass and immediately relates to the net force imposed on it (F=ma).
- **Third Law**: There is an equal and opposite response to every action.

Sound: The Nature of Acoustic Waves

Energy takes the form of sound, which is a pressure wave that moves through materials like water or air. Usually, it's expressed in decibels (dB). Though it moves through different media at different speeds, sound moves slower than light in most cases. Human hearing is based on the response of hair cells to pressure waves, which are then translated into electrical impulses that are transmitted to the brain. The waveform's frequency and amplitude, among other factors, dictate the qualities of sound, such as pitch and volume.

Electromagnetism: The Interplay of Electric and Magnetic Forces

A basic subject in physics is electromagnetic, which is the study of electric and magnetic fields and how they interact. Because protons, neutrons, and electrons are charged particles, atoms, which are made up of them, have electromagnetic properties. Neutrons are neutral, protons are positively charged, and electrons are negatively charged. Electric fields and forces are created when these charges interact.

- **Electric Currents and Fields**: The flow of electrons, or electric current, is measured in amperes (A). Electric currents generate magnetic fields, which can influence the velocity of charged particles. The force produced by electric fields is described by Coulomb's law, which associates the force with the product of the charges and inversely with the square of the distance between them.

Optics: The Science of Light

The area of physics known as optics studies the characteristics and behavior of light. Light is a wave-like and particle-like substance that is a part of the electromagnetic spectrum. Every color in the visible light spectrum has a matching wavelength and energy level, ranging from red (longer wavelengths) to violet (shorter wavelengths).

- **Behavior of Light**: One can absorb, reflect, or refractively bend light. Light energy is converted to heat through absorption, whereas light waves are changed in direction during reflection and refraction. When light strikes a surface, it reflects, and when it passes through various objects, it is refracted.

Heat: Energy in Transit

Energy is transferred from hotter to colder substances in the form of heat. It is expressed in joules or calories and is an expression of the innate energy that exists in all substances. Understanding the rules of thermodynamics and the processes involved in heat transport are essential to the study of heat.

- **Heat Transfer**: Convection, or fluid movement, radiation, or electromagnetic waves, and conduction, or direct touch, are the three ways that heat can be conveyed. Every technique has unique qualities and uses.

Magnetism: The Force of Moving Charges

The mobility of electric charges, mostly electrons, is what causes magnetism. Electron flow generates magnetic fields, especially in materials containing unpaired electrons. Both charged particles and other magnets are subject to these fields' forces.

- **Magnetic Fields and Forces**: Electric currents produce magnetic fields, which have the ability to affect electric charges. The fact that magnetic fields always form closed loops, leaving a magnet's north pole and entering its south pole, is one of their most important properties. Teslas (T) are units used to measure magnetic field strength.

Chemistry
Atomic Structure: The Building Blocks of Matter

Atoms are vital to all matter despite being exceedingly small. They are made up of an electron-surrounded nucleus. The center of an atom is known as the nucleus, and it includes protons and neutrons. Neutrons are neutral particles that add to the atom's mass without changing its charge, whereas protons have a positive charge. The amount of protons in the nucleus determines the atomic number, which is used to identify each element on the periodic table. For instance, carbon has six protons although hydrogen, the most basic element, only has one. Electrons orbiting the nucleus have distinct energy levels due to the negative charge. The arrangement of these electrons, particularly in the outermost shells, is crucial for the way atoms form bonds with one another. The configuration of an atom's electrons determines not only its chemical characteristics but also how reactive it is with other atoms, resulting in the creation of molecules and compounds.

Compounds: Chemical Combinations

Compounds are created when two or more elements combine chemically to provide unique qualities that set them apart from their component parts. There are two main ways that this bonding can happen: covalent and ionic. Atoms exchange electrons when they form covalent bonds, as in the case of water (H_2O), when two hydrogen atoms and one oxygen atom share electrons. Stable molecules can develop because of this sharing of electrons. Ionic bonding, on the other hand, is the process by which atoms exchange electrons to form electrically charged ions. Ionic compounds are created when these ions are drawn to one another by their opposing charges. A well-known example is sodium chloride (NaCl), a molecule that is necessary for numerous biological processes as a result of sodium (Na) giving an electron to chlorine (Cl).

Acids and Bases: Proton Donors and Acceptors

In the field of chemistry, bases and acids are essential. In chemical reactions, acids have the ability to donate a hydrogen ion (H+). They are well-known for corroding metals and having a tart flavor. In contrast, hydrogen ions are accepted by bases. They frequently have a slick texture and an unpleasant taste. In many chemical reactions, particularly neutralization reactions where they mix to generate water and a salt, the interaction of acids and bases is essential. The pH scale, which goes from 0 to 14, determines how basic or acidic a thing is. A pH of 7 or more is regarded as basic, whereas a pH of less than 7 is considered acidic. We discover neutral things like pure water around the halfway point of 7. This scale is essential for understanding the chemical makeup of different chemicals and their interactions in a wide range of scientific domains, including biology and environmental science.

Physical Changes: Alterations Without Identity Loss

A substance can undergo physical changes in its shape or appearance without experiencing a change in its chemical makeup. These alterations frequently entail reversibility and don't result in the creation of new compounds. The phase transitions of water, such as the change from solid to liquid that occurs when ice melts and the shift from gas to liquid that occurs when water vapor condenses, are common examples. A shift in physical state, not in chemical structure, is what happens in both processes. Additional instances of physical alterations include the shattering of a glass, the stretching of a rubber band, and the tearing of paper. Each time, the material's chemical composition stays the same, but its outward appearance varies.

States of Matter: Forms of Existence

The four main states of matter in the cosmos are solid, liquid, gas, and plasma. Every state has certain characteristics that define it:

- **Solid**: Matter keeps its volume and shape constant when it is in a solid state. Because the particles are arranged in a particular way and are not moving much, solids are incompressible and stiff. Metals, rocks, and ice are a few examples.
- **Liquid**: Although they have a set volume, liquids adopt the shape of their container. Liquids can flow because the particles in liquids are less firmly packed than in solids and can move around one another. Among the liquids are mercury, water, and oil.
- **Gas**: Neither the shape nor the amount of gaseous substances are fixed. Because their particles are widely dispersed and free to move, gases are extremely compressible. Airborne examples include carbon dioxide, nitrogen, and oxygen.
- **Plasma**: Since plasma is an ionized gas, it can carry electricity and has free electrons and ions in it. It is frequently

seen in settings with exceptionally high energy, such as stars, such as the sun. Although it is less widespread on Earth, plasma is still visible in plasma TVs and neon signs.

Chemical Changes: Transformations at the Molecular Level

Compounds undergo chemical reactions to generate new compounds with distinct properties, which causes chemical changes. Usually, these modifications are irreversible. For instance, when paper burns, it combines with the oxygen in the air to produce ash, carbon dioxide, and water vapor, so changing the composition of the air. Another example is rusting iron, in which iron combines with oxygen and water to create iron oxide, a novel material. Food undergoes complicated chemical reactions when it is cooked, which alters the food's flavor, color, and texture. These changes are essential for the synthesis of novel materials and chemicals in a variety of industries, including industrial manufacture and cooking.

ELECTRONIC INFORMATION

The purpose of the ASVAB test's Electronics Information portion is to assess your knowledge of fundamental electronic concepts and elements. This part covers a wide range of subjects, including the principles of electrical currents and conductors as well as the operation of wires and gauges. You have to fully comprehend these fundamental concepts in order to pass this segment of the test.

The electron flow theory, which describes how electrons flow through conductors, is one important topic of study. Negatively charged electrons normally move from a circuit's negative terminal, or anode, to its positive terminal, or cathode. This movement is dictated by the attraction and repulsion forces that exist between charged particles. Understanding the principles underlying atom structure is also crucial. Atoms are made up of protons, neutrons, and electrons. Neutrons, known as neutral particles, and protons, that are positively charged particles, make up an atom's nucleus. Negatively charged electrons circle the nucleus at different energies. Understanding the behavior and interactions of these subatomic particles is essential to comprehending ideas related to electricity.

Conductivity: Conductors, Semiconductors, and Insulators

Another important concept is conductivity, which is the ease with which electrons can travel through a material. Conductors are perfect for use in electrical circuits because they let electrons go freely and with little resistance, like copper. Rubber and other insulators, on the other hand, have high resistance and stop electron flow, which makes them safe for use in electrical applications.

Between conductors and insulators, semiconductors are in the middle. Temperature variations are one example of the conditions that can affect their conductivity. Heat causes semiconductors to become more conductive, in contrast to conductors. Semiconductor materials include graphite, which is frequently used in resistors.

Test Format and Preparation

The Electronics Information section examines your understanding of fundamental electrical terms throughout a large part of the course. It's critical that you understand the meanings of basic electrical terminology. This includes being aware of the definitions of terms like frequency, resistance, voltage, and current. If you can grasp these ideas, you will be able to apply and understand more complicated electrical principles.

This part has 15 questions that must be answered in 10 minutes for those taking the CAT-ASVAB, and 20 questions in 15 minutes for those using paper and pencil. In order to prepare well, make sure you have a thorough comprehension of the fundamentals by concentrating on the electronic information core principles. This strategy will provide you the skills you need to answer the vocabulary and real-world application questions in the ASVAB Electronics Information segment.

Electronics Information: Current, Voltage, and Resistance

- **Current**: The rate at which electric charges move across a conductor in a circuit is referred to as current. Amperes, which are coulombs per second, are used to measure it. Understanding current is essential to comprehending how electrical circuits work. Devices and systems are powered by these charges moving through them.
- **Voltage**: The force that moves electric charges over a circuit is known as voltage, or electric potential difference. It is equivalent to the force that accelerates the charges and is expressed in volts. In order to create current,

voltage is necessary; otherwise, the electric charges would remain static. Voltage is a relevant topic in electronics because of the variation in electric potential.

- **Resistance**: The characteristic of a material that prevents current passage is called resistance. It fluctuates based on the composition of the substance and is expressed in ohms. Electron flow is facilitated by conductors' low resistance and is impeded by insulators' high resistance. A material's atomic structure and physical dimensions define its resistance.

Circuits: The Pathways of Current

The operation of any electrical equipment depends on circuits. In essence, they are channels that permit the flow of electric current and carry out beneficial tasks. A voltage source, such as a battery or power supply, conductors, such as cables, and loads, such as resistors or light bulbs, are the fundamental parts of a circuit.

Types of Circuits

- **Series Circuits**: Components are connected sequentially along a single path in a series circuit. The same current passes successively through each component in this configuration. Similar to old-fashioned Christmas lights, where a single burned-out bulb would result in the entire string becoming dark, if one part of the circuit malfunctions or is disconnected, the entire circuit will stop working. $R_{total} = R_1 + R_2 + R_3 +...$ is the formula that can be used to compute the total resistance in a series circuit, where R_1, R_2, R_3,... are the resistances of individual components.
- **Parallel Circuits**: Components in parallel circuits are linked via junctions or common points, allowing the current to travel along several routes. In contrast to series circuits, a parallel circuit's constituent parts can still function even if one fails. This occurs as a result of each part being connected to the voltage source separately. In a parallel circuit, the resistance of each branch determines the current that flows through it, but the voltage across each branch remains constant. The formula $1/R_{total} = (1/R_1)+(1/R_2)+(1/R_3)+...$ can be used to compute the total resistance in a parallel circuit, which is less than the resistance of the smallest resistor.
- **Series-Parallel Circuits**: These circuits combine parallel and series design elements. They are utilized in more advanced electronic gadgets and are more complex. These circuits have certain parts connected in series and some connected in parallel. More control over the distribution of voltage and current among the various components of the circuit is possible with this configuration.

Electrical Power: The Work of a Circuit

A fundamental idea in electronics, electrical power is the speed at which electrical energy transforms into other forms of energy, such heat, light, or mechanical force. It is essential to the operation of electrical equipment and plays a crucial role in the planning, building, and assessment of electronic systems.

- **Calculating Electrical Power**: $P = V \times I$ is the formula most frequently used to calculate power in an electrical circuit. P, V, and I represent power (watts), voltage (volts), and current (amperes) respectively in this formula. This formula is based on the link between voltage, current, and energy in an electrical circuit as well as the fundamental notion of power, which is defined as energy per unit of time. $P = I^2 \times R$ and $P = V^2/R$, where R denotes resistance in ohms, are two more helpful formulas. When only two of the three variables—voltage, current, and resistance—are known, these formulas come in handy.
- **Importance of Electrical Power**: An electrical device's power rating tells you how much electricity it can handle or convert in a certain amount of time without failing or overheating. For example, a 60-watt lightbulb produces heat and light from 60 watts of electrical power. Designing an electrical system safely and effectively requires an understanding of power ratings.

Units and Measurements in Electronics

Accurate measurement is essential to the design, testing, and debugging of circuits in electronics. Anyone working in this profession has to be familiar with the standard units and their scaling.

- **Ohms**: Ohms are used to measure resistance (symbol: Ω). It measures the degree to which a substance resists the passage of electrical current. For a given voltage, less current flows through higher resistance.
- **Amperes**: Amperes, or amps, are used to measure current (symbol: A). It symbolizes the passage of an electric charge via a conductor. One coulomb of charge moving through a location in a circuit once every second is equal

to one ampere.

- **Volts**: The unit of measurement for voltage, or electric potential difference, is volts (symbol: V). It acts as the conduit for electric current and is comparable to plumbing water pressure.
- **Watts**: Watts are used to represent power in electrical circuits (symbol: W). It displays the energy transfer or conversion rate in proportion to time.
- **Metric Prefixes**: Because electronics components and circuits can have a wide variety of values, it is essential to understand metric prefixes. To illustrate, the symbols kilo- (k), mega- (M), and giga- (G) represent thousand, million, and billion units, respectively. On the other hand, one thousandth is represented by milli- (m), one millionth by micro- (μ), and one billionth by nano- (n).

Household Electrical Systems: Essentials for Safety and Functionality

Understanding the fundamentals of electricity, such as the distinctions between AC and DC currents and the significance of grounding, is essential for practical application and safety in the context of home electrical systems.

AC vs. DC Currents

- **Direct Current (DC)**: The unidirectional flow of electric charge is what defines DC. DC, which is frequently produced by batteries, is necessary for low-voltage applications like those found in automobiles and electrical equipment. Resistance is the main issue with DC circuits because it obstructs the flow of current.
- **Alternating Current (AC)**: Conversely, AC is defined by its alternating flow direction. This kind of current is commonly produced by alternators and is used to supply homes and businesses with power. Impedance, which comprises reactance and resistance, is a key factor in influencing the behavior of AC circuits.

Frequency in AC Circuits

An important parameter for an AC waveform is its frequency, which is expressed in hertz (Hz). It shows how many cycles a waveform completes in a single second. For example, a frequency of 60 Hz, which is typical for residential electrical systems in North America, indicates that the current reverses direction 60 times per second.

$f = 1/T$ represents the link between frequency (f) and one cycle's time period (T). This relationship is essential to comprehending and creating AC circuits, particularly in the context of electronics, where frequencies can vary from gigahertz (GHz) to DC (0 Hz).

Grounding in Electrical Systems

Earthing, also known as grounding, is a safety precaution that involves connecting an electrical system to the earth in order to neutralize excess charge. This procedure gives the system's voltages a reference point and aids in stabilizing voltage levels.

A home's electrical systems require ground wires. They provide a low-resistance channel to the ground, which is essential in the event of a circuit fault or surge to avoid electric shocks and damage to electrical appliances.

Resistors: Essential Components in Circuit Design

Resistance is a key concept in electronics, especially while studying for the ASVAB exam. Essential parts of electrical circuits, resistors are mainly employed to modify voltage levels and regulate current flow.

Function and Identification of Resistors

Resistors are passive components; that is, they control power rather than producing it. They play a crucial role in determining how circuits behave by regulating the amount of current that passes through different parts. Usually, resistors can be identified using color-coded bands. These bands represent the resistor's tolerance and resistance value. The color bands are used to compute the resistance value, with each color denoting a different number or multiplier.

If the resistivity of a resistor's material is known, its resistance can be ascertained. $R = rho \times (L/A)$ is the formula used to compute resistance, where (rho) stands for resistivity, (L) for length, and (A) for cross-sectional area. This formula helps explain how resistance is affected by material qualities and physical dimensions.

Types of Resistors

- **Fixed Resistors**: The resistance value of these resistors is always the same. There are three types: wire-wound (built with wire on an insulating form), metal film (made with a metal alloy or carbon film), and carbon composition (made from carbon and clay).

- **Variable Resistors**: Resistance can be changed with these resistors within a predetermined range. They are employed in applications such as volume controls that call for frequent adjustments. Variable resistors are available in different power ratings and can be built from a variety of materials.

Potentiometers and Rheostats

- A potentiometer is a kind of variable resistor that has three terminals and may be adjusted to change resistance in different ways. It serves as a voltage divider frequently.
- Rheostats are used to control high-power applications, such as dimming lights. They usually have two terminals. Compared to potentiometers, they have larger power ratings and can be wire-wound.

Circuit Protection: Fuses and Circuit Breakers

In electrical circuits, circuit breakers and fuses are essential safety components. By cutting the circuit, they guard against power overloads, averting possible harm or dangers.

A short circuit happens when the current unintentionally follows a shorter path than intended, which causes the current to surge. This can be hazardous, which is why fuses and circuit breakers are essential in averting such incidents.

Capacitors and Their Role in Circuits

Capacitors are just as important in the world of electronics as resistors and inductors. Their primary function is to supply temporary electrical energy storage inside a circuit. Because of its capacity for storage, capacitors can continue to hold a charge even when they are cut off from a voltage source—just like a battery that is losing energy.

Capacitor Structure and Function

Typically, a dielectric—a non-conductive substance—separates two conducting plates in a capacitor. The capacitor's structure allows it to hold electrical charge. The formula $C = Q/V$, where (C) is capacitance, (Q) is the stored charge, and (V) is the applied voltage, is used to determine a capacitor's capacitance, or measure of its capacity to hold charge. Farads (F) are used to express capacitance.

Capacitive Reactance in AC Circuits

Capacitive reactance is a special kind of impedance that capacitors show in circuits that use alternating current (AC). The frequency of the AC signal and the capacitance of the capacitor have a negative correlation with each other. It is calculated using $X_c = 1/\omega C$, where (omega) is the angular frequency.

Semiconductors and Their Applications

Materials classified as semiconductors can function as insulators or conductors based on factors like doping and temperature. Two common semiconductors are silicon and germanium.

- **Doping Process**: Doping is the process of changing a semiconductor's electrical characteristics by introducing impurities. The material's conductivity can be changed by this method, improving its suitability for a range of electrical applications.
- **Diodes**: N-type and P-type materials are fused together to generate semiconductor diodes. Because they let current to flow in one direction while obstructing it in the other, they are essential for processes like rectification, or the conversion of AC to DC. There are two states for diodes: reverse-biased, which blocks current flow, and forward-biased, which permits current passage. The cathode (negative) and anode (positive) are essential for figuring out which way the current is flowing.

Transistors: Amplifiers and Switches

In circuits, transistors—three-terminal semiconductor devices—are utilized to switch and amplify electrical signals.

Types of Transistors

NPN transistors are made up of two N-type layers sandwiched by a thin P-type layer. They are extensively employed in switching and amplification applications.

Since transistors have a thin N-type layer positioned between two P-type layers, they operate similarly to NPN transistors but with distinct types of charge carriers.

Transistor Components

- A transistor's base serves as the control terminal, controlling the movement of charge carriers.
- From the emitter to the collector, where charge carriers are gathered, the current flows.
- The transistor starts working when the emitter releases charge carriers.

Exploring Electricity and Magnetism

Two essential components of electromagnetic, a powerful force in physics, are electricity and magnetism. Gaining an understanding of these ideas is necessary to comprehend the fundamentals of how different electronic systems and gadgets operate.

1. **Magnetic Field Dynamics**: Electric charges, such as electrons circling atomic nuclei or electric currents flowing through wires, produce magnetic fields. Conducting wires are wound around a core material to form electromagnets. As current flows across these wires, a magnetic field is produced.
2. **The Role of Inductors**: Electrical circuit inductors are passive parts that are usually made of a wire coil wound around a magnetic core. When an electric current passes through them, they retain energy in a magnetic field. When the flow of current varies, inductors oppose it by producing an opposing electromotive force (EMF). This characteristic, referred to as inductance, is especially important in circuits that use alternating current (AC).
3. **Transformers**: Voltage Conversion Devices: Transformers are employed in electrical circuits to modify the voltage levels. They are made up of a common core encircled by two coils, primary and secondary. Which way the transformer steps up or down in voltage depends on how many turns there are in the main coil compared to the secondary coil.
4. **Motors and Generators**: With electric motors, electrical energy is converted to mechanical energy. Usually, they are made of an electric current-driven, rotating wire loop in a magnetic field. By rotating a coil inside of a magnetic field, generators use the electromagnetic induction principle to transform mechanical energy into electrical energy.
5. **Mastering Ohm's Law**: A fundamental concept in electronics, Ohm's Law $I = \frac{V}{R}$, establishes a relationship between current (I), voltage (V), and resistance (R). Comprehending and utilizing this law is essential for resolving a variety of electrical issues.

AUTO AND SHOP INFORMATION

The ASVAB test's Auto and Shop Information portion dives deeply into the nuances of car mechanics and the equipment used in automotive workshops. You will gain an understanding of the many systems and parts of automobiles, as well as the equipment and procedures used in auto maintenance and repair, by following this thorough tutorial. The ASVAB tests your knowledge of shop tools and vehicle components by combining auto and shop themes. Each component of the test, Auto Information and Shop Information, has a different amount of questions and a time limit.

Understanding Vehicle Mechanics

The engine transforms the chemical energy of gasoline into mechanical energy for propulsion, much like the heart of an automobile. Cars with internal combustion engines are commonplace. The burning of gasoline produces heat, which is then transformed into mechanical force.

An internal combustion engine's essential parts are as follows:

- **Camshaft**: Regulates when the fuel intake and exhaust gas expulsion valves open. Engine efficiency is affected by variations such as overhead cam (OHC) and overhead valve (OHV) designs.
- **Combustion Chamber**: The location where air and gasoline combine to burn and produce power for the engine.
- **Connecting Rod**: Causes linear motion to be converted into rotating motion by connecting the piston and

crankshaft.

- **Crankshaft**: turns the pistons' up-and-down activity into circular motion in order to move the car.
- **Cylinders**: Contains the pistons; an engine's power and characteristics are determined by the number of cylinders.
- **Cylinder Head**: Seals the fuel injectors, spark plugs, housing valves, and top of the cylinder.
- **Engine Block**: The central framework that houses the engine's essential parts.
- **Exhaust Valve**: Allows the combustion chamber's exhaust gasses to escape.
- **Intake Valve**: Controls how much fuel and air enters the combustion chamber.
- **Pistons**: Compress the air-fuel combination and capture combustion energy by moving within the cylinders.
- **Wrist Pins**: Fit the pistons with the connecting rods.

Understanding the Mechanics of Engine Operation

The four strokes that make up an internal combustion engine's cycle of operation are intake, compression, combustion (or power), and exhaust. Every stroke in the engine's cylinders signifies a distinct action that adds to the overall energy conversion process.

1. **Intake Stroke**: As the piston descends, a vacuum is created and fuel and air pass through the engine's cylinder through the intake valve.
2. **Compression Stroke**: The fuel-air mixture is compressed as the piston rises, increasing its density and potential energy.
3. **Combustion/Power Stroke**: The spark plug ignites the mixture near the top of the compression stroke, triggering an explosive expansion that pushes the piston downward and produces mechanical energy.
4. **Exhaust Stroke**: The cylinder is ready for the subsequent intake cycle when the piston rises once more, releasing the combustion byproducts through the exhaust valve.

Cylinder Configurations in Engines

An engine's cylinder arrangement can change, which can affect the engine's size, balance, and performance. Inline, V, flat, and radial designs are examples **of common installations.**

1. **Inline** Engines: These engines, which are typically seen in cars with fewer cylinders, are characterized by a linear layout of cylinders and are renowned for their simplicity and balance.
2. **V Engines**: These engines are ideal for high-performance and larger cars because of their compact design and ability to accommodate more cylinders. They have two angled cylinder banks that form a 'V' shape.
3. **Flat (Boxer) Engines**: Although they may need extra width area, flat engines with horizontally opposed cylinders have a low center of gravity and smooth operation.
4. **Radial Engines**: Radial engines, which have cylinders arranged in a circle around the crankshaft and are known for their compact design and excellent power-to-weight ratio, have historically been employed in airplanes.

Cylinder Firing Order: The Rhythm of Power Generation

The precise order in which each cylinder ignites its mixture of gasoline and air is known as the engine's firing order. This order is essential for preserving engine balance, reducing vibrations, and maximizing efficiency. Smooth operation and an even distribution of power are guaranteed by a well-planned firing sequence.

There are several firing orders for different engine setups. For example, 1-3-4-2 is a typical firing sequence for inline-4 engines, which guarantees a balanced and smooth running. Because of their natural balance, inline-6 engines may run in the 1-5-3-6-2-4 sequence. The distinct firing orders of V6 and V8 engines, such as 1-2-3-4-5-6 or 1-8-4-3-6-5-7-2, are intended to improve performance and lessen vibrations.

How Diesel Engines Differ

The way that diesel engines, also known as compression-ignition engines, ignite is different from that of gasoline engines. They do not require spark plugs since they ignite the gasoline using the heat produced by compressing the air in the cylinder. When diesel fuel is pumped into the cylinder, the compressed air in the engine raises its temperature to a degree where it ignites the fuel. This procedure demonstrates the diesel engines' power and efficiency.

Essentials for Effective Engine Operation

1. **Air-Fuel Mixture**: For combustion, the air-fuel combination is essential. Complete combustion is ensured by the stoichiometric ratio, which is normally approximately 14.7:1 for gasoline engines. Variations in this ratio impact performance and emissions by producing lean (more air) or rich (more fuel) mixes.

2. **Ignition Timing**: Ignition time in gasoline engines refers to the exact instant the spark plug ignites the mixture of fuel and air. Precise timing is essential for maximum power and effectiveness. This matches the fuel injection time in diesel engines.

3. **Combustion**: The process through which the fuel and air mixture burn and release energy is called combustion. Significant engine damage can result from abnormal combustion events including pre-ignition or detonation (engine knocking).

In-Depth Exploration of Automotive Cooling and Lubrication Systems

The Cooling System: Maintaining Engine Temperature

- **Types of Cooling Systems**: While some older or specialty models may use air-cooled systems, most modern vehicles use liquid-cooled systems. The design, intended use, and performance needs of the vehicle are some of the elements that influence the decision between liquid-cooled and air-cooled systems.

- **Components and Functioning**: A water-antifreeze mixture known as coolant is pumped through the engine by the liquid-cooled system. Heat from the engine is taken up by this coolant and transferred to the radiator, where it is circulated after being cooled by airflow. The water pump, radiator, thermostat, and coolant hoses are important parts that are all essential to this heat exchange process.

- **Maintenance and Care**: To avoid overheating and engine damage, the cooling system must receive routine maintenance. This involves making sure the radiator and pipes are in excellent shape, monitoring the coolant levels, and looking for leaks. For best results, the system must be flushed on a regular basis and the right coolant type must be used.

The Engine Lubrication System: Reducing Friction and Wear

- **Types of Lubrication Systems**: Cars usually have a dry sump or wet sump lubrication system. While the dry sump system employs an external tank to provide improved oil control, particularly in high-performance scenarios, the wet sump system stores oil in a pan at the base of the engine.

- **Key Components and Their Roles**: Maintaining the health and performance of a vehicle requires an understanding of the functions of the numerous parts that make up the lubrication system. Let's examine these crucial components' roles in more detail:

  1. **Oil Pan (Sump)**: Located at the base of the engine is the oil pan, often known as the sump. In the off-road mode, it acts as a storage container for engine oil. The oil pan's capacity and design are very important since they guarantee that there will always be enough oil to lubricate the engine, regardless of driving circumstances or angle.

  2. **Oil Pump**: The oil pump is the hub of the lubrication system. It takes oil out of the oil pan and uses pressure to force it through the engine's lubricating circuit. Even with different engine speeds and temperatures, the pump makes sure that all important engine components receive a steady supply of oil. The engine design might affect the kind of oil pump (gear, rotor, or vane) and where it is located (internal or exterior).

  3. **Oil Filter**: The oil filter, which is positioned along the oil circuit, is essential to preserving the purity of the oil. By clearing the oil of impurities like soot, metal fragments, and dirt, it keeps engine parts from wearing down abrasively. Usually, the filter is made of synthetic or paper filtration media. To avoid blockages and preserve oil flow and cleanliness, it is imperative to replace the oil filter on a regular basis.

  4. **Oil Galleries (Passages)**: A system of channels that are cast or drilled into the cylinder head and engine block is known as an oil gallery. These channels transmit the pressurized oil from the pump to the valve train, pistons, crankshaft and camshaft bearings, and other engine parts. These galleries' layout makes sure that oil effectively lubricates and reduces wear on every component of the engine.

  5. **Pressure Relief Valve**: A safety measure that keeps high oil pressure from harming seals, gaskets, and other engine parts is the pressure relief valve. This valve, which is either inside the oil pump or close to it, opens when the oil pressure rises above a predetermined point, allowing extra oil to skip the filtration system and

return straight to the sump. This system makes sure that the oil pressure is constant under all engine circumstances.

6. **Additional Components**: Additional parts, such as secondary filters and oil coolers, may be found in more sophisticated engines. Oil coolers are beneficial in preserving the ideal oil temperature, particularly in heavy-duty or high-performance engines. Magnetic filters and other secondary filters offer an additional line of defense against metallic pollutants.

- **Engine Oil, the Lifeline of the Lubrication System**: The kind and quality of engine oil are vital to engine health. It aids in cleaning and sealing, lowers friction, and cools engine parts. For optimal outcomes, the viscosity of the oil, as indicated by SAE ratings, should correspond with the manufacturer's standards. To withstand increased operating stresses, diesel engines need oil that has been carefully prepared.

Understanding the Combustion Systems in Automobiles

Transporting gasoline from the tank to the engine and maintaining a balanced fuel and air mixture for optimal engine performance is the main responsibility of the fuel system. To improve engine performance, this system also filters contaminants out of the gasoline, keeps the fuel pressure at its ideal level, and modifies fuel supply depending on the driving situation.

Types of Fuel Systems

1. **Carburetor System**: An older fuel system device called a carburetor blends gasoline and air before it reaches the engine. It adjusts the fuel flow according to the air intake. The proper operation of carburetors requires routine maintenance.

2. **Electronic Fuel Injection System**: This contemporary technology precisely delivers fuel to the engine through the use of electrical sensors and a computer. Compared to carburetor systems, it offers better fuel economy and reduced emissions by continually monitoring and adjusting the air-to-fuel ratio.

Components of the Fuel System

- **Electric Fuel Pump**: It is situated next to the gasoline tank and is powered by the powertrain control module (PCM) to pump fuel to the engine.
- **Fuel Filter**: It is positioned along the fuel lines to filter contaminants out of the fuel and guarantee that the engine receives clean fuel.
- **Fuel Rail**: A channel that delivers gasoline to the injectors while sustaining steady pressure and flow.
- **Fuel Pressure Regulator**: controls fuel pressure and fuel entry according to engine demand.
- **Fuel Injectors**: Fuel is sprayed into the engine cylinders under PCM control for maximum efficiency.
- **Intake Manifold**: Transfers the combination of air and fuel to the engine cylinders, improving performance.
- **Intake Air Filter**: Eliminates contaminants from the air prior to it entering the engine.
- **Powertrain Control Module (PCM)**: The fuel distribution system's computer modifies it to provide the best possible engine performance.
- **Throttle Body/Plate**: Controls the engine's intake of air by reacting to input from the accelerator pedal.

Fuel Injection Systems

- **Throttle Body Injection (TBI)**: a more basic setup with a single injector that is frequently seen in older cars.
- **Multiport Fuel Injection (MFI)**: offers increased performance and economy by using several injectors for each cylinder.
- **Direct Injection**: usually found in more recent versions, sprays fuel directly into the combustion chamber for improved performance and efficiency.

Maintaining the fuel system on a regular basis is essential. This include checking that the gasoline tank is clean, cleaning the intake manifold and throttle body, and replacing the fuel filter. Frequent checks by a trained technician can avert serious problems and preserve the longevity and effectiveness of the system.

Ignition System

In automobiles, the ignition system is essential for starting the fuel-air combination in the combustion chamber of the engine. With time, this system has evolved to include cutting-edge technology that improve power output and efficiency.

The primary system, which produces the high voltage required for fuel ignition, is where the ignition system's trip starts. This system is made up of various essential parts:

- **Battery**: This rechargeable unit supplies the initial electrical charge for engine startup and powers various electrical components when the engine is off.
- **Ignition Switch**: Activating the vehicle's electrical system, this switch triggers the engine's startup process and controls power distribution to accessories.
- **Primary Coil Winding**: Acting as an electromagnet, this coil, when energized, induces a high voltage in the secondary coil, initiating the spark for combustion.
- **Ignition Module**: This electronic component regulates the spark's timing and strength, ensuring optimal engine performance.
- **Regulator and Pickup Coil**: These elements work together to maintain appropriate voltage levels and signal the ignition module for precise spark timing.
- **Distributor**: This part transfers the high voltage between the coil and the proper spark plug at the appropriate moment in older systems.

The main working principle of the primary system is electromagnetic induction, which generates a high-voltage surge in the secondary coil and directs it toward the spark plugs.

The Secondary Ignition System: Distributing Power

The secondary system takes over from the primary system, channeling the high voltage to the spark plugs. Its components include:

- **Secondary Coil Winding**: This coil amplifies the voltage received from the primary coil.
- **Coil Wire**: It connects the coil to the distributor cap.
- **Distributor Cap and Rotor**: These allow the proper spark plug wire to receive the high voltage.
- **Spark Plug Wires**: These wires carry the high voltage to the spark plugs.
- **Spark Plugs**: The final components that create the necessary sparks for fuel combustion.

In operation, the secondary system ensures the delivery of electrical energy to the spark plugs, igniting the fuel mixture efficiently.

Advancements in Ignition Technology

Recent technological advancements have led to more efficient ignition systems, such as:

1. **Distributorless Ignition System (DIS)**: This modern system uses sensors to determine the crankshaft and camshaft positions, directly triggering the ignition coil. It offers a more consistent spark, enhancing engine performance and reliability.
2. **Coil-on-Plug (COP) Ignition**: Placing an ignition coil directly atop each spark plug, this system eliminates the need for spark plug wires and distributors. It provides a stronger spark, improving fuel efficiency and reducing emissions.

The automobile industry's continuous dedication to improving vehicle performance, fuel efficiency, and emissions reduction is reflected in these advances. Ignition systems are expected to advance in sophistication as technology does, enhancing both vehicle dependability and the driving experience.

Enhancing Vehicle Performance: The Role of Exhaust Systems

Within the field of vehicle mechanics, the exhaust system is essential for effectively eliminating engine exhaust fumes and reducing dangerous pollutants. This system, which is made up of numerous interrelated parts, makes sure that the car runs smoothly and complies with regulations regarding the environment. The performance of the exhaust system depends on a number of essential parts, each of which plays a specific role:

- **Exhaust Manifolds**: These are the conduits that gather exhaust gases from the engine's cylinders, funneling them into a single path leading to the rest of the exhaust system.
- **Catalytic Converter**: A pivotal element in emission control, the catalytic converter transforms harmful pollutants like carbon monoxide and nitrogen oxides into less hazardous gases, significantly reducing the vehicle's environmental impact.
- **Muffler**: The muffler, which is essential to noise reduction, muffled sound waves made by the engine's exhaust gases, making driving quieter and more enjoyable.
- **Tailpipe**: Serving as the exhaust system's exit point, the tailpipe discharges the treated exhaust gases into the atmosphere, strategically directing them away from the vehicle to prevent cabin infiltration.
- **Header Pipes**: These pipes connect the exhaust manifold to the catalytic converter. Their design is optimized to enhance exhaust flow, thereby boosting engine efficiency and performance.

How the Exhaust System Operates

Exhaust gases are gathered from each cylinder at the manifold, where their journey starts. After passing via the header pipes into the catalytic converter, these gasses undergo a chemical change that lessens their toxicity. The fumes then pass via the muffler, which muffles the sound of the engine, and out the tailpipe into the atmosphere.

Regular maintenance is essential to the exhaust system's lifetime and efficiency. Essential procedures include routinely checking for leaks, replacing worn-out parts on time, and cleaning the exhaust pipes to avoid deposit buildup. To prevent physical harm to the system, it is also advised to drive cautiously, particularly in unpaved or uneven areas.

Auto: Electrical and Chassis Systems - A Comprehensive Overview

The electrical and chassis systems are unique among the constantly changing parts of contemporary cars, as they guarantee both functionality and safety. These systems have experienced major changes, moving from mechanical to electrical functions, and they include a number of subsystems that are essential to the functioning of the vehicle.

The intricate electrical systems in cars are necessary for igniting the engine and providing power to several other systems.

- **Battery**: Serving as the backbone, the car battery is a lead-acid unit that converts chemical energy into electrical energy. It powers the starter motor and other electrical components, initiating the engine's operation.
- **Starting System**: This system harnesses the battery's energy to activate the starter motor, which in turn ignites the engine, setting the stage for autonomous operation.
- **Charging System**: Essential for powering the vehicle's electrical components, the charging system, led by the alternator, transforms mechanical energy from the engine into electrical energy, replenishing the battery.
- **Lighting System**: Comprising various interior and exterior lights, this system enhances visibility and safety. Controlled by switches, it includes protective measures like fuses or circuit breakers to prevent overheating and potential hazards.
- **Computer System**: Acting as the vehicle's nervous system, it includes the electronic control unit (ECU), sensors, and actuators. The ECU coordinates the operation of various systems, while sensors and actuators execute specific actions based on the ECU's signals.

Chassis Systems: The Foundation of Vehicle Dynamics

The drivetrain, suspension, steering, and brakes are all part of the chassis systems, and they all affect how well the car handles and performs overall.

- **Drivetrain System**: The transmission of power from the engine to the wheels is handled by this system. It encompasses multiple drivetrain configurations, such as front-wheel drive, rear-wheel drive, all-wheel drive, and four-wheel drive, as well as different transmission types, such as manual and automatic.
- **Transmission Types**:
  1. **Automatic Transmission**: Common in the US, it uses planetary gear sets for different gear ratios and a torque converter for power transmission.
  2. **Manual Transmission**: Requires manual engagement and disengagement of gears using a clutch pedal and gear shifter.
- **Drivetrain Types**:
  1. **Front-Wheel Drive (FWD)**: Features both the engine and drive wheels on the front axle, common in small

and compact vehicles.

2. **Rear-Wheel Drive (RWD)**: Has the powertrain on the front axle and drive wheels on the rear, typical in luxury sedans and sports cars.
3. **All-Wheel Drive (AWD)**: Delivers power to all four wheels constantly, adapting to various driving conditions.
4. **Four-Wheel Drive (4WD)**: Similar to AWD, it distributes power to all four wheels, often selectable by the driver, suitable for off-road conditions.

Drivetrain Components:

1. **Clutch**: Controls power and speed in manual transmissions.
2. **Constant-Velocity (CV) Joints**: Used in FWD and AWD vehicles for smooth power transfer.
3. **Differential**: Balances wheel rotation speed, crucial in RWD and many AWD vehicles.
4. **Drive Axle**: Transmits power from the differential to the wheels in RWD vehicles.
5. **Drive Shaft**: Connects the transmission output shaft to the differential input shaft.
6. **Half Shaft**: Transfers power from the differential to the wheels in FWD and AWD vehicles.
7. **Transaxle**: Combines transmission and axle functionalities, common in FWD vehicles.
8. **Transfer Case**: Used in 4WD and AWD vehicles to distribute power to front and rear axles.
9. **Transmission**: Regulates gear ratios, available in manual and automatic variants.
10. **Universal Joints**: Allow for power transmission between misaligned shafts.

Auto: Suspension, Steering, and Brake Systems

Knowing the nuances of the suspension, steering, and brake systems is essential for anyone working in the automotive industry. These systems are essential to a car's performance, comfort, and safety. Let's examine these systems in more detail, focusing on their parts and functions.

Suspension and Steering: Ensuring Stability and Control

The suspension and steering systems are made up of different components that work together to keep the car stable and make driving pleasurable.

- **Springs and Shock Absorbers**: The springs of the suspension system are its fundamental component and are usually composed of coiled steel. They facilitate smooth wheel movement and sustain the weight of the car. In order to preserve tire-road contact, shock absorbers work in tandem with springs to absorb and dissipate energy.
- **Control Arms and Bushings**: The control arms of the vehicle are connected to the steering knuckle by means of a capital 'A'-shaped connector. They preserve alignment while facilitating wheel movement. Bushings stabilize and cushion these connections; they are typically composed of rubber or polymer.
- **Steering Knuckle and Ball Joints**: One essential element that joins the suspension and steering components is the steering knuckle. It enables wheel pivoting, which is necessary for directional adjustments in a vehicle. Ball joints offer a variable pivot point that facilitates seamless suspension and steering operation.
- **Steering Linkage**: This system, often employing a rack and pinion design, connects the steering wheel to the steering knuckle. It includes tie rods and control arms, transmitting steering wheel movements to the wheels.
- **Wheel Hub**: The wheel hub is a central part of the wheel assembly, connecting the wheel to the suspension system and ensuring smooth wheel rotation.

Tires: The Vehicle's Contact with the Road

Tires are usually made of rubber and available in a variety of styles. Radial tires have been the most popular since the 1940s. Important tire parts include:

- **Beads and Rim**: Beads, made of steel wire, secure the tire to the rim, which is the wheel's outer edge.
- **Body Plies and Sidewalls**: These form the tire's main structure, with sidewalls sealing the air and protecting the plies.
- **Tread and Belts**: The tread is the rubber part contacting the road, while belts between the plies and tread stabilize the tire's footprint.

For maximum safety and performance, tires must be properly maintained, which includes routine inspections, rotations, and pressure adjustments.

Brake System: Ensuring Safe Stops

The brake system's primary role is to safely and effectively stop the vehicle. Its major components include:

- **Brake Pedal and Master Cylinder**: The brake pedal activates the brakes, transmitting force to the master cylinder, which generates hydraulic pressure for the braking process.
- **Brake Fluid Reservoir and Lines**: The reservoir stores brake fluid, while lines transport it to the wheel brakes.
- **Brake Assemblies**: Located at each wheel, these assemblies contain brake pads or shoes that create friction to slow or stop the vehicle.

Enhancing Braking: Power Brakes and ABS

1. **Power Brakes**: These systems use a brake booster to amplify the force applied to the brake pedal, reducing the effort needed to stop the vehicle.
2. **Anti-Lock Brake System (ABS)**: ABS prevents wheel lock-up during hard braking, maintaining vehicle control. It adjusts brake pressure based on wheel speed sensor inputs, enhancing safety during emergency stops.

Shop: Essential Measuring Tools in Automotive and Workshop Settings

Even with the introduction of sophisticated technology, traditional hand tools are still quite important in the automobile and workshop industries. These tools are still vital parts of a mechanic's toolbox because of their basic design, manual operation, and simplicity.

- **Calipers**: Calipers stand out as versatile instruments for gauging distances or diameters, with two primary types frequently **utilized in workshops:**
  1. **Outside** Calipers: These instruments are made to measure an object's exterior dimensions. They feature two legs extending from a central body, which are adjusted to match the size of the item being measured.
  2. **Inside Calipers**: Contrasting with outside calipers, these are tailored for internal measurements. The legs are repositioned to fit inside the item, branching out from a central point.

Both types of calipers have legs for measurement and a friction joint, allowing the tool to maintain its set position.

- **Micrometer**: The micrometer, often referred to as a micrometer screw gauge, is renowned for its precision in measuring external dimensions.
  1. **Spindle and Anvil**: The spindle, a cylindrical part, moves towards or away from the anvil, enclosing the object for measurement.
  2. **Sleeve and Thimble**: The sleeve, marked for measurements, remains stationary, while the thimble, also marked, is rotated to adjust the spindle's position.
- **Spirit Levels**: Spirit levels, or bubble levels, are indispensable for verifying the horizontality (level) or verticality (plumb) of surfaces.
  1. **Tubular Spirit Levels**: These contain a curved glass tube with a liquid and a bubble, indicating the levelness of a surface.
  2. **Bullseye Spirit Levels**: Circular in design, they function similarly to tubular levels but can assess levelness in multiple directions simultaneously.
- **Steel Squares**: A steel square, crucial for precise measurements and drawing straight lines, consists of two parts:
  1. **Blade**: The longer arm, marked with measurements, is used for drawing and measuring straight lines.
  2. **Tongue**: The shorter arm, at a right angle to the blade, is also marked for measurements.
- **Tape Measure**: A tape measure, with its flexible ribbon marked with linear measurements, is a staple in both professional and DIY settings. Its versatility in measuring size or distance is unmatched.
- **Steel Rule**: For more precise measurements over shorter lengths, a steel rule is preferred. This rigid, flat steel tool, marked along its length, is ideal for drawing straight lines and taking accurate measurements.

Shop: The Essentials of Striking and Fastening Tools

Tool indispensables in the realm of mechanical work: striking and fastening tools. These instruments are mostly used to apply force or join materials together. A variety of hammers, fasteners, and other hitting instruments that are frequently seen in a workshop are covered in this section.

- **Hammers**: Hammers are one of the most ancient and universally used hand tools, available in diverse types for a range of tasks.

1. **Ball-Peen Hammer**: This hammer, with a flat face for striking and a rounded end for shaping metal, is a staple in metalworking and mechanical applications.
2. **Rubber or Wooden Mallet**: Ideal for delivering gentle blows, these mallets are used in woodworking, automotive assembly, and sheet metal shaping, ensuring no damage to the material.
3. **Claw Hammer**: Primarily for driving and pulling out nails, it features a flat head for striking and a claw for nail removal. A rough framing hammer, similar but heavier, is used in construction for driving large nails.
4. **Sledge Hammer**: With a long handle and heavy head, it's designed for delivering powerful blows, useful in demolition and driving stakes.

- **Fasteners**: Fasteners like nails and rivets are crucial for joining materials.
1. **Nails**: Common in construction, nails have a head for hammering, a shank for grip, and a point for penetration. They vary in size and type, each suited for specific uses.
2. **Rivets**: The cylindrical shaft of these permanent mechanical fasteners has a head on it. Used for joining metals, they are hammered or pressed to create a second head, securing the materials together.

Additional Striking Tools

Other striking instruments that are necessary for fine work include drifts, punches, and chisels. These implements are made to withstand blows from a hammer and convert the force into useful motions.

- **Chisels**: Used for carving or cutting materials like wood or metal, chisels are driven by a hammer or mallet. Cold chisels, made for cutting unheated metals, are a specific type.
- **Punches**: Tools like pin punches and center punches are used for driving or marking materials. They are struck by a hammer to perform their function.
- **Drifts**: Made from softer metals, drifts are used for aligning or enlarging holes. They are struck with a hammer and are common in automotive repair and metalworking.

Turning Tools

Fasteners and hardware like bolts, nuts, and screws are handled with turning tools.

- **Screwdrivers**: Designed for screws, they come in various types like flathead, Phillips, Robertson, and Torx, each matching a specific screw head.
- **Wrenches**: Used for applying torque to turn nuts and bolts, wrenches come in forms like open-end, box-end, combination, and adjustable wrenches.
- **Sockets**: Fitting over nuts and bolts, sockets attach to a socket wrench handle and come in sizes like six-point and twelve-point.

Bolts and Nuts: The Threaded Pair

Bolts and nuts are threaded fasteners typically used together. Bolts pass through materials and are secured with a nut on the other side.

- **Thread Pitch**: The thread pitch gauge measures the distance between a bolt or screw's threads.
- **Fractional Measurement Fasteners**: Bolts and nuts measured in fractions of an inch, common in the imperial system.
- **Nuts**: Used with bolts, nuts come in various types like hex nuts, wing nuts, castellated nuts with cotter pins, and lock nuts.

Shop: The Art of Joining and Welding

The ability to join and weld materials is essential in the mechanical field. This section examines the equipment and methods for welding and fastening, emphasizing their value in a range of applications.

Fastening with Precision: Ring Fasteners and Soldering

- **Ring Fasteners**: Also known as retaining rings or snap rings, these mechanical fasteners are essential in securing components onto shafts or within housings. They come in two types:
1. **Internal Snap Rings**: Designed to fit inside a bore or housing.

2. **External Snap Rings**: Made to fit over a shaft.
Both types are instrumental in controlling the position of assemblies and preventing lateral movement.
- **Soldering**: A fundamental process in electronics, plumbing, and metalwork, soldering involves joining materials using a melted filler metal, known as solder. There are different types of solder:
  1. **Lead-Based Solder**: Common due to its low melting point and cost-effectiveness, though environmental concerns have led to alternatives.
  2. **Silver Solder**: Known for its strength and higher melting point, suitable for high-temperature applications.
  3. **Copper Solder**: Chosen for its excellent electrical conductivity and corrosion resistance.
- **Preparation and Tools**: Preparing for soldering includes cleaning surfaces and applying flux, a chemical agent that aids in soldering. The primary tools are the soldering iron and soldering gun, each with unique features for specific tasks.

The World of Welding: Techniques and Safety
- **Welding**: A process that joins materials by melting them together, welding is widely used in construction, automotive manufacturing, and more.
  1. **Oxyacetylene Welding**: Utilizes a flame from a gas mixture to melt base metals, with a filler rod for joint filling.
  2. **Electric-Arc Welding**: Employs an electrical current to create an arc that melts metals at the welding point.
- **Stick Welding**: This is a common manual arc welding technique that makes use of a flux-coated consumable electrode. Key components include:
  1. **Stinger**: Holds the welding electrode and conducts current.
  2. **Welding Rod**: The consumable electrode that melts to form the weld.
  3. **Flux**: Coats the welding rod, shielding the weld area from atmospheric gases and forming protective slag.
- **Metal Inert Gas (MIG) Welding**: MIG welding is effective and adaptable, and it is distinguished by the continuous wire electrode that is fed through a welding gun.
- **Protective Equipment**: Safety in welding is paramount. Essential gear includes a welding helmet, safety glasses, welding jacket, gloves, and boots, each designed to protect against the hazards of welding.

Shop: Mastery of Gripping and Cutting Tools
The capacity to grip, cut, and manipulate materials is crucial in the field of mechanical work. This section explores the several types of grasping and cutting tools that are essential in any workshop, emphasizing the special uses and capabilities of each one.

Gripping Tools: Holding and Manipulating with Precision
- **Pliers**: Pliers are indispensable tools in any workshop, designed for gripping, bending, twisting, and cutting. They come in various forms:
  1. **Combination Slip-Joint Pliers**: These adjustable pliers are versatile, featuring a slip joint for size adjustment, flat and curved gripping areas, and a cutting edge.
  2. **Adjustable Joint Pliers**: Known as tongue-and-groove pliers, they feature an adjustable jaw for gripping objects of varying sizes, ideal for plumbing tasks.
  3. **Channellock® Pliers**: The main function of these adjustable pliers is to hold and rotate nuts and bolts.
  4. **Lineman Pliers**: Essential for electricians, these pliers combine gripping and cutting functions, ideal for wire work.
  5. **Diagonal Cutters**: Designed specifically for cutting wire, their angled cutting edge allows for precision.
  6. **Needle-Nose Pliers**: With their long, slender tips, they are perfect for reaching into tight spaces and precise wire bending.
  7. **Vise-Grip® Pliers**: Locking pliers that can function as pliers, a wrench, or a clamp, offering versatility and hands-free operation.
- **Clamps**: Essential for securing objects, clamps are widely used in carpentry and metalworking. The C-clamp, with its C-shaped frame, is a popular choice for its versatility.
- **Vises**: A mechanical instrument called a vise is used to hold objects precisely in place. It has two parallel jaws that

are moveable and fixed, enabling precise work on the object.

Cutting Tools: Shaping and Slicing with Accuracy
- **Manual Saws**: Traditional hand-operated saws, each designed for specific materials and cuts:
  1. **Crosscut Saw**: Ideal for cutting wood perpendicular to the grain.
  2. **Rip Saw**: Designed for cutting along the wood grain.
  3. **Coping Saw**: Perfect for intricate shapes and interior cut-outs in woodworking.
  4. **Backsaw**: a sharp instrument used in conjunction with a miter box to make precise cuts.
  5. **Hacksaw**: Primarily for cutting metal, featuring a strong, adjustable frame.
- **Power Saws**: Electric saws that reduce manual labor, each suited for different tasks:
  1. **Circular Saw**: Versatile and portable, ideal for straight cuts.
  2. **Miter Saw**: Specialized for making angled cuts.
  3. **Table Saw**: Excellent for precise, straight cuts in woodworking.
  4. **Band Saw**: Ideal for curved cuts and intricate shapes.
- **Drilling and Boring Tools**: Essential for creating and enlarging holes:
  1. **Drill Bits**: Used to remove material and create holes, available in various sizes and shapes.
  2. **Hole Saws**: Designed for cutting larger holes in thin materials.
  3. **Electric Drill**: A versatile tool for drilling holes and driving fasteners, available in corded and cordless models.

Finishing Tools: Refining and Perfecting the Work
- **Planes**: Used to flatten or shape wood, planes like the jack plane are crucial for both rough shaping and fine finishing.
- **Wood Chisels**: Essential for detailed wood carving and shaping.
- **Files and Rasps**: Files remove fine amounts of material for a smooth finish, while rasps are used for more aggressive material removal, especially in woodworking.

MECHANICAL COMPREHENSION

The Mechanical Comprehension section of the ASVAB test evaluates your grasp of basic mechanical principles and devices. While technical terminology isn't always necessary, a fundamental understanding of mechanics is crucial, especially for specific roles in the military.

Exploring Mechanical Principles
- **Mass and Matter**: Mass is the quantity of matter in an object, independent of gravity. Everything that has mass and requires up space is considered matter.
- **Force**: Forces, which can be thought of as pushes or pulls, are interactions between objects. They have both magnitude and direction. All of the forces operating on an object add up to zero when its velocity is unchanged.
- **Gravity**: This force of attraction between masses is described by the equation $F_g = G(m_1 \times m_2)/r^2$. Gravity, which pulls objects towards Earth, is always attractive.
- **Friction**: Opposing the motion of objects, friction arises from surface interactions and is always in the opposite direction of movement.
- **Compression and Tension**: Compression is an inward force, like a squeeze (calculated as force divided by area), while tension is a pulling force, measured in pounds or Newtons.

Newton's Laws of Motion
1. **First Law (Inertia)**: Absent an external force, an object continues to be at rest or move uniformly.
2. **Second Law**: Mass and acceleration are inversely related to one another, with force being equal to mass times acceleration.
3. **Third Law**: Every action has an equal and opposite reaction.

Fluid Dynamics: Air and Water Pressure
- **Air Pressure**: Influenced by gravity, air pressure is greater closer to Earth's surface due to denser atmosphere.
- **Water Pressure**: Increases with depth, as more water weight exerts force per unit area.
- **Hydraulic Lifts**: Utilize incompressible fluids to transmit force, following the equation $A_1 \times D_1 = A_2 \times D_2$, where A is the cross-sectional area and D is the distance traveled by the fluid.

Filling and Emptying Tanks
It is crucial to concentrate on calculating flow rates and comprehending the interaction between inflow and outflow rates when addressing issues involving the filling and emptying of tanks. The secret to fixing these issues is figuring out how much fluid is left in the tank after a given amount of time. The formula Final Volume = Initial Volume + (Inflow Rate - Outflow Rate) x Time is used to accomplish this. Where:
- **Final Volume** is the amount of fluid in the tank at the end of the given period.
- **Initial Volume** is the amount of fluid at the beginning of the period.
- **Inflow Rate** is the rate (in liters per hour, for example) at which the fluid enters the tank.
- **Outflow Rate** is the speed at which the liquid exits the reservoir.
- **Time** is the duration over which the inflow and outflow occur.

Using this method, you may determine how much fluid is left in the tank after a specific amount of time, accounting for both incoming and outgoing fluid. Through comprehension and utilization of this equation, one can proficiently ascertain the fluid dynamics in a tank under a variety of conditions, including filling, emptying, or a mixture of the two.

Torque: The Twist in Mechanics
The amount of twisting force applied to an object is measured as torque. It's an important idea to grasp how forces result in rotational movement. Force multiplied by distance equals torque.

Understanding Work, Energy, and Power in Physics
Fundamental ideas in physics are work, energy, and power, each of which denotes a different facet of physical processes. These scalar values are essential to comprehending forces and motion mechanics because of their magnitude and lack of a directional component.

Work: The Force-Displacement Product
The application of a force over a specific distance is known as work in physics. It is computed by multiplying the force acting on an item by the object's displacement in the force's direction. The Joule, which is comparable to a Newton-meter, is the unit of work.

Work is calculated as follows: Work = Force x Distance.

Positive or bad work outcomes are possible. When the force and displacement are moving in the same direction, positive work is produced; when they are moving in different directions, negative work is produced.

For example, if you apply a force of 10 Newtons to move a table 5 meters, the work done is:

Work = 10N x 5 m = 50J

Energy: The Capacity to Do Work
In essence, energy is the capacity for labor. It can be transformed into labor in any of its many forms.

Potential plus kinetic energy adds up to the total mechanical energy in a system free from nonconservative forces (such as friction):

PE plus KE equals E_{total}.

The work performed by non conservative forces is also included in the total energy if they exist:

PE + KE + $W_{external}$ force equals E_{total}.

Kinetic Energy: Motion-Related Energy
The energy that an object has as a result of motion is known as kinetic energy. The formula for it is $KE = (1/2)mv^2$, where m and v stand for mass and velocity, respectively. Joules are also used to quantify kinetic energy.

The kinetic energy change of an object and the amount of work done on it are equal, according to the work-energy theorem.

Potential Energy: Position-Based Energy
Potential energy is connected to an object's position or configuration. Different types of energy exist, including gravitational, elastic, and electrical potential energy. $U_g = mgh$ is the formula for gravitational potential energy, where mass (m), gravitational acceleration (g), and height above a reference point (h) are expressed. An object's potential energy grows with its height.

Other Energy Forms
- **Chemical Energy**: Found in molecular bonds, releasing or absorbing energy during bond formation or breakage.
- **Electric Energy**: Associated with moving electrons or electric current.
- **Nuclear Energy**: Derived from atomic nuclei alterations.
- **Solar Energy**: Originating from the sun's light and heat.

Power: Work Over Time
The rate at which energy is transmitted or work is completed is measured by power. It is measured in watts (joules per second) and is defined as work completed per unit of time.

$P = W/t$ is the formula for power.

Exploring Mechanical Motion and Mechanical Advantage
We examine the dynamics of several mechanical systems, such as crank-piston mechanisms, spinning wheels, pulleys, gears, and cams, in the study of mechanical motion. Mechanical advantage (MA), or the increase in force attained by using machinery, is a fundamental idea in this field.

A machine can magnify an applied force thanks to the idea of mechanical advantage. It is computed by contrasting the force attained (load) with the force applied (effort).

For example, a mechanical advantage of 10 is obtained when a 100N object is lifted by a 10N force. When distances are involved, the following formula can be used to determine MA:

Load distance / Effort distance = MA

Simple Machines: Utilizing Mechanical Advantage
Basic devices known as simple machines use mechanical advantage to accomplish tasks. These consist of wheels and axles, levers, pulleys, screws, inclined planes, wedges, and gears.
- **Gears**: The ratio of the driven gear's teeth to the driving gear's teeth determines the mechanical advantage of a gear system. For example, a 20-tooth gear driven by a 5-tooth gear has an MA of 4.
- **Inclined Planes**: These devices distribute work over a longer distance, easing the effort needed to move an object. The MA is the ratio of the slope's length to its vertical rise.
- **Levers**: Levers fall into three kinds, each distinguished by a unique configuration of the fulcrum, load, and effort. The MA of a lever is the ratio of the effort distance to the load distance, or the load force to the effort force.
- **Pulleys**: The MA of a pulley system is the ratio of the effort distance to the load distance. The number of ropes sustaining the weight in a system with numerous ropes is equal to the MA.
- **Screws**: The MA of a screw is found by comparing the effort distance (2π times the length of the tool used to turn the screw) to the load distance (the distance the screw travels in one turn).
- **Wedges**: The MA of a wedge, like an axe, is the ratio of its length to its width or height.
- **Wheel and Axle**: In these systems, the MA is the ratio of the radius of the effort (like a screwdriver handle) to the radius of the load (the screwdriver blade).

Understanding Compound Machines and Structural Mechanics
Within the field of mechanics, compound machines are important. In essence, these are assemblages made up of several simple machines. The mechanical advantages of each individual simple machine in the assembly must be calculated, and these values must then be multiplied together to provide the overall mechanical advantage (MA) of a compound machine.

Take into consideration, for example, a compound machine that consists of three basic machines, each having a mechanical advantage of 5, 2, and 1. The sum of these separate MAs would equal the compound machine's total mechanical advantage:

10 is MA_{total} (5 x 2 x 1).

Structural Support: Balancing Strength and Distribution

An essential component of engineering is structural support, which focuses on the quantity and distribution of supports inside a building. This idea can be used in a variety of contexts, such as the construction of structures and bridges, or the distribution of weight among people carrying an object.

For instance, each of the four carriers bears an equal portion of the weight if it is divided equally among them. On the other hand, if the weight is closer to one person, then that person bears a larger share. Similar to this, the strength and distribution of supports are essential for stability and load-bearing capacity in constructions like bridges.

Properties of Materials: Conductivity, Flexibility, and Malleability

Different materials exhibit distinct properties due to their inherent composition. Key properties include:

- **Heat Conduction**: This characteristic relates to a material's ability to transport heat. Metals, for instance, are excellent conductors of heat, whereas plastics are less efficient.
- **Flexibility**: This defines the capacity of a material to bend without breaking and revert to its initial shape. Springs are highly flexible, while glass is not.
- **Malleability**: Malleability is the ease with which a material can be reshaped. Materials like clay or dough are highly malleable, but they lose this property once hardened.

The Physics Connection: Fundamental Understanding

mastery the mechanical interactions of particular things is more important for comprehending mechanical principles than having a thorough mastery of physics terms. The operation of levers, pulleys, gears, and pistons must be understood.

Force (force = mass × acceleration), action/reaction, equilibrium, pressure, kinds of force (friction, gravity, magnetism, recoil, static electricity), work, and energy are important physics concepts to review. Basic mathematical procedures are necessary for certain topics, but not all of them necessitate formulaic computations.

Tips for Mechanical Comprehension Success

When tackling the Mechanical Comprehension section of the ASVAB test, keep these tips in mind:

1. The force required to move an object is never more than the object's weight, excluding frictional resistance.
2. Eliminate answers that lack a mechanical basis. If an answer doesn't mechanically explain the problem, it's likely incorrect.
3. Changes in mechanical operations often have both positive and negative consequences. Look for answers that reflect this balance, such as those involving increases and decreases or gains and losses.

Comprehending these concepts will not only facilitate success on assessments such as the ASVAB, but also furnish a fundamental understanding beneficial in an array of technical and engineering domains.

ASSEMBLING OBJECTS

The Armed Services Vocational Aptitude Battery (ASVAB) Assembling Objects component is meant to evaluate your spatial skills. This entails putting an object's many components together visually. This section is especially pertinent to some Navy missions where spatial awareness is essential. In seventeen minutes, candidates must answer fifteen multiple-choice questions with illustrations. Connection items and puzzle items are the two main categories into which the questions are divided.

Understanding Connection Items

You are challenged to mentally connect lines and shapes using connection items. In these questions, there are several shapes and lines that have attachment points indicated by letters next to them. For example, you could see a triangle with the letter "B" at one end and "A" at the other, or a square with a "A" indicated at a certain location. Your job is to mentally put these parts together by matching the letters, then choose the right assembled image from the list of possibilities.

It could be necessary for you to mentally shift or rotate the parts in these items, but flipping or mirroring them is not necessary. A reflected piece is a common trap that can be included in some erroneous options even though they appear correct. It's similar to perfectly fitting a jigsaw puzzle piece, which needs to be rotated but not flipped.

Puzzle Items: Creating a New Shape

In puzzle objects, you have to put together different forms to create a new, whole shape. You have to mentally arrange the many forms that you'll be given to fit into one of the supplied options. Similar to connection objects, these forms can be moved or rotated but not mirrored. All original shapes must be used, and no new ones may be added.

For instance, you might be required to put together a collection of geometric forms to create a new shape. All of the provided forms must be used in the right number and orientation in the right response. The ability to manipulate and link shapes mentally is necessary for this.

Effective Strategies for Solving Assembling Objects Questions

To handle both connection and puzzle parts correctly, it helps to approach them carefully. Focus on one component at a time when working on puzzles, and make sure you cross-check your solution with the list of possible answers to eliminate incorrect responses. Similarly, for the connection items, carefully examine the shapes to ensure that the designated points match the correct location in the answer choices.

The ASVAB's part on object visualization and manipulation in space looks at this skill. For many technical and engineering jobs in the armed forces, this is a crucial ability. You can do far better on this test section if you develop an acute sense of detail and practice your mental rotation and shape assembly.

CHAPTER 5 - PRACTICE TESTS, SOLUTIONS, AND ANALYSIS

ARITHMETIC REASONING

Welcome to our thorough ASVAB Study Guide's "Arithmetic Reasoning" chapter. This chapter is an essential part of the fifth major section, "Practice Tests, Solutions, and Analysis," which is intended to provide you with the knowledge and skills you need to do well on the ASVAB test.

We explore the core of mathematical thinking in this section, which is a key component of the ASVAB exam. Our method is designed to simulate the real exam experience by giving you a set of questions that are similar to what you would get on test day. These aren't just any old math questions; instead, they've been thoughtfully designed to capture the tone, intricacy, and variety of the arithmetic reasoning section of the ASVAB.

You will come across a range of questions in this chapter that test your comprehension and application of mathematical ideas. These questions will assess your ability to use mathematical ideas to address real-world problems. They range from straightforward computations to more complicated circumstances needing critical thinking and problem-solving skills.

There is a thorough solutions section at the end of the chapter. This is a thorough examination and explanation of every issue, not just a list of the right responses. The purpose of this section is to help you better comprehend the ideas and methods required to solve arithmetic reasoning problems. Through these explanations, you will be able to identify typical mistakes and discover effective strategies for solving different kinds of arithmetic problems.

This chapter will help you improve your mathematical thinking abilities, which are crucial for the ASVAB as well as many other facets of daily life. It's not just a study guide for the test. We urge you to carefully consider each question and use the solutions area to hone your problem-solving skills and expand your comprehension.

Let this chapter serve as your guide as you confidently and curiously set out on this trip to conquer the arithmetic reasoning section of the ASVAB.

1. If you multiply 7 by 9 and then multiply 9 by 7, according to the Commutative Property of Multiplication, will the results be the same, different, or undefined?
    a) The same
    b) Different
    c) Undefined

d) Cannot be determined without additional information

2. When dividing 144 by 12, what is the quotient, and does this division result in any remainder?
a) 12, with no remainder
b) 12, with a remainder of 1
c) 13, with no remainder
d) 11, with a remainder of 1

3. What is the result of subtracting -5 from -10?
a) -15
b) -5
c) 5
d) 15

4. Which of the following numbers is a prime number?
a) 21
b) 22
c) 23
d) 24

5. Which of the following is a factor of 36?
a) 8
b) 9
c) 11
d) 14

6. What is the Least Common Multiple (LCM) of 6 and 8?
a) 12
b) 24
c) 48
d) 36

7. Which of the following is an example of an improper fraction?
a) 3/4
b) 4/3
c) 1/2
d) 2/5

8. How can the fraction 20/60 be reduced to its lowest terms?
a) 1/3
b) 1/2
c) 2/3
d) 3/4

9. Convert the fraction 3/4 into a decimal.
a) 0.75
b) 0.25
c) 0.50
d) 0.33

10. What is the product of multiplying 0.5 by 0.2?
a) 0.10
b) 0.07

c) 1.0

d) 0.02

11. What is the value of 3 raised to the power of 4 (3^4)?

a) 81

b) 64

c) 27

d) 12

12. What is the square root of 49?

a) 7

b) 9

c) 6

d) 8

13. What is the factorial of 5 (5!)?

a) 120

b) 60

c) 24

d) 30

14. Convert 5 miles to kilometers, knowing that 1 mile is approximately 1.60934 kilometers.

a) 8.0467 kilometers

b) 7.5468 kilometers

c) 3.21868 kilometers

d) 6.045 kilometers

15. What is the volume of a cube with three meters for each side?

a) 27 cubic meters

b) 9 cubic meters

c) 12 cubic meters

d) 6 cubic meters

16. In a set of numbers 3, 7, 9, 12, and 14, what is the median value?

a) 7

b) 9

c) 10

d) 12

17. How likely is it to land on heads when a fair coin is flipped?

a) 1/2

b) 1/3

c) 1/4

d) 2/3

18. If 4 gallons of paint cover 100 square feet, how many gallons are needed to cover 250 square feet?

a) 6 gallons

b) 10 gallons

c) 8 gallons

d) 2.5 gallons

19. What is 30% of 150?

a) 45

b) 50
c) 55
d) 60

20. If a car's value decreases from $20,000 to $15,000 over a year, what is the percent change?
a) 25% decrease
b) 20% decrease
c) 30% decrease
d) 15% decrease

21. What number comes after 2, 4, 8, 16, and so on?
a) 18
b) 20
c) 32
d) 24

22. Convert the fraction 3/5 to a percentage.
a) 60%
b) 55%
c) 65%
d) 50%

23. What is the average velocity of a vehicle that covers 300 miles in 5 hours?
a) 60 mph
b) 55 mph
c) 65 mph
d) 50 mph

24. If the quantity of a product doubles when the price halves, this is an example of what kind of proportion?
a) Direct proportion
b) Inverse proportion
c) Complex proportion
d) Linear proportion

25. What is the result of the following operation: 8 + 2 * 5?
a) 50
b) 18
c) 40
d) 30

26. If the probability of rain on any given day is 0.3, what is the conditional probability of it raining given that it is cloudy, assuming the probability of rain when cloudy is 0.8?
a) 0.24
b) 0.56
c) 0.4
d) 0.7

27. In a set of data, if the range is large, what does this indicate about the spread or dispersion of the data?
a) The data points are very similar.
b) The data points are widely spread out.
c) The data is inconsistent.
d) The data cannot be analyzed.

28. What is the average of the numbers 20, 30, and 50?
   a) 30
   b) 31
   c) 35
   d) 40

29. What is the area of a rectangle that is 10 meters long and 5 meters wide?
   a) 50 square meters
   b) 15 square meters
   c) 25 square meters
   d) 30 square meters

30. What is the logarithm of 1000 to the base 10 (log10 1000)?
   a) 2
   b) 3
   c) 4
   d) 5

1. Answer: a) The same
Explanation: According to the Commutative Property of Multiplication, the outcome is independent of the sequence in which the operations are performed. Therefore, 7 x 9 and 9 x 7 both yield the same product, which is 63.

2. Answer: a) 12, with no remainder
Explanation: Dividing 144 by 12 results in a quotient of 12 without any remainder, as 144 is exactly divisible by 12.

3. Answer: c) 5
Explanation: A negative number can be added to its positive equivalent by subtracting it. Therefore, -10 - (-5) is the same as -10 + 5, which equals -5.

4. Answer: c) 23
Explanation: A prime number is any number bigger than 1 that has just itself and 1 as its just positive divisors. So it can only be divisible properly by 1 and 23, 23 is a prime number.

5. Answer: b) 9
Explanation: A number is said to be a factor if it divides into it without producing a remainder. 9 is a factor of 36 because 36 divided by 9 equals 4, with no remainder.

6. Answer: b) 24
Explanation: Among two integers, the smallest number that is a multiple of both is their Least Common Multiple (LCM). The LCM of 6 and 8 is 24, as it is the smallest number that both 6 and 8 can divide into without a remainder.

7. Answer: b) 4/3
Explanation: A fraction is considered improper if the denominator (bottom number) equals or exceeds the numerator (top number). 4/3 is an improper fraction as 4 is greater than 3.

8. Answer: a) 1/3
Explanation: Divide the fraction by its greatest common divisor in order to get the lowest terms possible for the numerator and denominator. 20 and 60 are both divisible by 20, so 20/60 reduces to 1/3.

9. Answer: a) 0.75
Explanation: Division of the numerator by the denominator produces the decimal corresponding of the fraction. 3 divided by 4 equals 0.75.

10. Answer: a) 0.10

Explanation: Multiplying decimals involves multiplying the numbers as whole numbers and then placing the decimal point. 0.5 x 0.2 equals 0.10.

11. Answer: a) 81

Explanation: Exponents represent repeated multiplication. 3 raised to the power of 4 (3^4) means 3 multiplied by itself 4 times: 3 x 3 x 3 x 3, which equals 81.

12. Answer: a) 7

Explanation: A number that gives its initial value when multiplied by itself is known as a number's square root. The square root of 49 is 7, as 7 x 7 equals 49.

13. Answer: a) 120

Explanation: The sum of all positive integers that equal the specified value is its factorial. 5! (5 factorial) is 5 x 4 x 3 x 2 x 1, which equals 120.

14. Answer: a) 8.0467 kilometers

Explanation: To convert miles to kilometers, multiply the number of miles by the conversion factor (1 mile = 1.60934 kilometers). 5 miles x 1.60934 equals approximately 8.0467 kilometers.

15. Answer: a) 27 cubic meters

Explanation: One way to compute a cube's volume is to cube one of its sides' lengths. A cube with sides of 3 meters has a volume of 3 x 3 x 3, which equals 27 cubic meters.

16. Answer: b) 9

Explanation: The middle value in the arranged sequence of values is identified as the median. In the set 3, 7, 9, 12, and 14, when arranged in ascending order, 9 is the middle number.

17. Answer: a) 1/2

Explanation: A fair coin has two sides, heads and tails, making the probability of landing on heads 1 out of 2, or 1/2.

18. Answer: b) 10 gallons

Explanation: If 4 gallons cover 100 square feet, then to cover 250 square feet, which is 2.5 times more area, you need 2.5 times more paint. So, 4 gallons x 2.5 = 10 gallons.

19. Answer: a) 45

Explanation: 30% of 150 is calculated by multiplying 150 by 0.30 (30/100). This equals 45.

20. Answer: a) 25% decrease

Explanation: The percent change is calculated by the formula: [(Final Value - Initial Value) / Initial Value] x 100. Here, [(15000 - 20000) / 20000] x 100 = -25%, indicating a 25% decrease.

21. Answer: c) 32

Explanation: The sequence is doubling each number. Thus, after 16, the next number is 16 x 2 = 32.

22. Answer: a) 60%

Explanation: Take the top number, divide it by the bottom number, and multiply the result by 100 to get the percentage of a fraction. So, (3/5) x 100 = 60%.

23. Answer: a) 60 mph

Explanation: The calculation of average speed involves dividing the whole distance by the total time. Here, 300 miles / 5 hours = 60 mph.

24. Answer: b) Inverse proportion

Explanation: A situation of inverse proportion arises when one value rises while the other falls. Here, as the price halves (decreases), the quantity doubles (increases).

25. Answer: b) 18

Explanation: According to the order of operations, multiplication is done before addition. So, 2 * 5 = 10, and then 8 + 10 = 18.

26. Answer: a) 0.24

Explanation: Conditional probability is calculated as $P(A|B) = P(A \text{ and } B) / P(B)$. Here, P(rain and cloudy) = 0.3, and P(cloudy) = 0.8. So, 0.3 / 0.8 = 0.24.

27. Answer: b) The data points are widely spread out.

Explanation: A large range in a data set indicates that there is a wide spread between the smallest and largest values, meaning the data points are widely spread out.

28. Answer: c) 35

Explanation: The average is calculated by adding all numbers and dividing by the count of numbers. (20 + 30 + 50) / 3 = 100 / 3 = 33.33, which rounds to 35.

29. Answer: a) 50 square meters

Explanation: The length multiplied by the breadth of a rectangle equals the area of that shape. 10 meters x 5 meters = 50 square meters.

30. Answer: b) 3

Explanation: The logarithm of 1000 to the base 10 is the power to which the base must be raised to produce 1000. 10^3 = 1000, so $\log_{10} 1000$ = 3.

WORD KNOWLEDGE

1. Choose the word that best fits the definition: "To make something less severe or serious."
   a) Aggravate
   b) Alleviate
   c) Intensify
   d) Provoke

2. What is the synonym of "Candid"?
   a) Deceptive
   b) Frank
   c) Secretive
   d) Unclear

3. Which word means "to confirm or give support to"?
   a) Undermine
   b) Corroborate
   c) Contradict
   d) Dispute

4. Select the word that means "extremely bad or appalling."
   a) Atrocious

b) Mediocre
c) Pleasant
d) Admirable

5. What is the antonym of "Benevolent"?
a) Kind
b) Generous
c) Malevolent
d) Compassionate

6. Choose the word that best fits the definition: "Lacking in variety and interest."
a) Monotonous
b) Exciting
c) Diverse
d) Fascinating

7. Which word means "to make a situation worse"?
a) Exacerbate
b) Ameliorate
c) Improve
d) Alleviate

8. Select the word that means "showing a lack of experience, wisdom, or judgment."
a) Naive
b) Experienced
c) Astute
d) Shrewd

9. What is the synonym of "Ephemeral"?
a) Permanent
b) Fleeting
c) Enduring
d) Infinite

10. Select the term that most closely matches the definition: "Unaffected by sentiments or personal beliefs when evaluating and presenting the facts".
a) Biased
b) Subjective
c) Objective
d) Prejudiced

11. Which word means "to express disapproval of"?
a) Praise
b) Condone
c) Censure
d) Endorse

12. Select the word that means "capable of working successfully; feasible."
a) Viable
b) Impossible
c) Impractical
d) Unworkable

13. What is the antonym of "Prosaic"?
a) Dull
b) Ordinary
c) Imaginative
d) Mundane

14. Pick the term that most closely matches the definition: "Having or exhibiting an insignificant or low estimate of one's value."
a) Arrogant
b) Humble
c) Boastful
d) Pretentious

15. Which word means "to recover quickly from a difficult condition"?
a) Deteriorate
b) Languish
c) Resilient
d) Succumb

16. In the sentence "The doctor's prognosis for the patient's recovery was optimistic," what does the word 'prognosis' imply?
a) A medical procedure
b) A prediction of the likely outcome
c) A detailed report
d) A prescription for medication

17. What does the prefix 'dis-' in the word 'disagree' suggest about the word's meaning?
a) To agree strongly
b) To agree partially
c) Not to agree
d) To agree again

18. The word 'unearth' most nearly means:
a) To bury
b) To discover
c) To clean
d) To cover up

19. In the word 'submarine,' the prefix 'sub-' most likely means:
a) Above
b) Beyond
c) Under
d) Across

20. What does the suffix '-ful' in the word 'joyful' indicate about the word's meaning?
a) Without joy
b) Full of joy
c) Beyond joy
d) Before joy

21. The word 'bicycle' contains the root word 'cycle.' What does 'cycle' mean in this context?
a) Speed
b) Wheel

c) Path

d) Seat

22. In the sentence "Her actions were counterproductive to the team's success," what does 'counterproductive' mean?

a) Highly productive

b) Opposite of productive

c) Somewhat productive

d) Equally productive

23. What does the root word 'therm' in 'thermometer' refer to?

a) Pressure

b) Light

c) Heat

d) Weight

24. The prefix 'inter-' in the word 'interact' suggests what about the word's meaning?

a) Act before

b) Act alone

c) Act between

d) Act again

25. In the word 'independent,' what does the prefix 'in-' mean?

a) Without

b) Within

c) Before

d) After

26. What does the suffix '-logy' in the word 'biology' suggest about the word's meaning?

a) The study of

b) The fear of

c) The love of

d) The history of

27. In the context of the sentence "The novel's protagonist was a paragon of virtue," what does 'paragon' mean?

a) A rival

b) A model of excellence

c) A minor character

d) A typical example

28. The word 'microscope' contains the root word 'scope.' What does 'scope' mean in this context?

a) Small

b) Instrument for viewing

c) Detailed

d) Long

29. What does the prefix 'auto-' in the word 'autobiography' imply about the word's meaning?

a) Written by another

b) Written about cars

c) Self or own

d) Written in the past

30. In the word 'rejuvenate,' what does the prefix 're-' indicate about the word's meaning?
   a) To make young again
   b) To make old
   c) To make worse
   d) To make permanent

1. Answer: b) Alleviate
Explanation: "Alleviate" means to make something less severe or serious, typically referring to pain, distress, or difficulties.

2. Answer: b) Frank
Explanation: In speech or writing, "Frank" is a synonym for "open, honest, and direct," whereas "Candid" refers to being truthful and straightforward.

3. Answer: b) Corroborate
Explanation: The word "corroborate" refers to providing evidence or support for a claim, hypothesis, or discovery.

4. Answer: a) Atrocious
Explanation: "Atrocious" means extremely bad or appalling, often used to describe something unpleasant or of poor quality.

5. Answer: c) Malevolent
Explanation: "Benevolent" means well-meaning and kindly. Its antonym is "malevolent," which denotes wanting to harm other people.

6. Answer: a) Monotonous
Explanation: "Monotonous" describes something that is uninteresting, monotonous, and repetitive.

7. Answer: a) Exacerbate
Explanation: "Exacerbate" means to make a problem, bad situation, or negative feeling worse.

8. Answer: a) Naive
Explanation: "Naive" means showing a lack of experience, wisdom, or judgment, often implying a certain innocence or simplicity.

9. Answer: b) Fleeting
Explanation: "Ephemeral" means lasting for a very short time; "Fleeting" is a synonym that also refers to something that passes quickly.

10. Answer: c) Objective
Explanation: "Objective" refers to the absence of subjectivity or prejudice in the consideration and representation of facts; it is the opposite of subjective or biased.

11. Answer: c) Censure
Explanation: "Censure" means to express severe disapproval of someone or something, typically in a formal statement.

12. Answer: a) Viable
Explanation: "Viable" means capable of working successfully or feasible, often used in the context of plans, methods, or ideas.

13. Answer: c) Imaginative
Explanation: "Prosaic" refers to the prose-like diction and style, devoid of lyrical beauty; lacking poetic beauty. "Imaginative" is its antonym, meaning having or showing creativity or inventiveness.

14. Answer: b) Humble
Explanation: "Humble" is the antithesis of arrogant or pretentious; it refers to having or displaying a humble or low assessment of one's importance.

15. Answer: c) Resilient
Explanation: "Resilient" means able to withstand or recover quickly from difficult conditions, showing toughness and perseverance.

16. Answer: b) A prediction of the likely outcome
Explanation: 'Prognosis' refers to a forecast or prediction, particularly in a medical context. It does not imply a procedure, report, or prescription.

17. Answer: c) Not to agree
Explanation: The prefix 'dis-' often means 'not' or 'the opposite of.' Therefore, 'disagree' means to not agree.

18. Answer: b) To discover
Explanation: 'Unearth' literally means to dig up from the earth, but it is commonly used to mean discovering something hidden or lost.

19. Answer: c) Under
Explanation: The prefix 'sub-' means under or below, as in 'submarine,' which operates under the water.

20. Answer: b) Full of joy
Explanation: The suffix '-ful' means full of. Therefore, 'joyful' means full of joy.

21. Answer: b) Wheel
Explanation: The root word 'cycle' refers to a circle or wheel, as in 'bicycle,' which means a vehicle with two wheels.

22. Answer: b) Opposite of productive
Explanation: 'Counterproductive' means having the opposite effect of productivity, hindering or negating progress.

23. Answer: c) Heat
Explanation: The root word 'therm' refers to heat, as in 'thermometer,' an instrument for measuring temperature or heat.

24. Answer: c) Act between
Explanation: The prefix 'inter-' means between or among, as in 'interact,' which means to act in relation to others.

25. Answer: a) Without
Explanation: The prefix 'in-' in 'independent' means not or without, indicating freedom from dependence.

26. Answer: a) The study of
Explanation: The suffix '-logy' denotes a field of study or academic discipline, as in 'biology,' the study of life.

27. Answer: b) A model of excellence
Explanation: 'Paragon' means a model or example of excellence or perfection.

28. Answer: b) Instrument for viewing
Explanation: The root word 'scope' refers to seeing or viewing, as in 'microscope,' an instrument for viewing small objects.

29. Answer: c) Self or own
Explanation: The prefix 'auto-' means self or own, as in 'autobiography,' a biography written by the person it is about.

30. Answer: a) To make young again

Explanation: Prefix 're-' frequently denotes again or back, as in the word 'revitalize,' which implies to rejuvenate or return youthful vitality.

PARAGRAPH COMPREHENSION

1. In 1987, the Great Wall of China, one of the world's greatest wonders, was added to the UNESCO World Heritage list. It winds up and down across meadows, mountains, plateaus, and deserts, resembling a massive dragon. It spans roughly 21,196 kilometers from east to west throughout China.

What is the primary purpose of the passage?
a) To describe the physical appearance of the Great Wall of China.
b) To argue for the preservation of the Great Wall of China.
c) To provide a historical account of the Great Wall of China.
d) To explain the construction techniques of the Great Wall of China.

2. Light energy is converted into chemical energy by plants and other living things through a process known as photosynthesis. Later on, this energy is released to power the organism's operations.

In light of the scripture, what is photosynthesis' primary purpose?
a) To produce oxygen for the atmosphere.
b) To convert light energy into chemical energy.
c) To help plants grow taller.
d) To absorb carbon dioxide from the environment.

3. Due to 'colony collapse disorder,' which has been connected to a number of issues like pesticides, habitat degradation, and parasites, the honeybee—an essential pollinator—is in immediate danger.

What is the passage primarily concerned with?
a) The life cycle of honeybees.
b) The economic value of honeybees.
c) The threats faced by honeybees.
d) The process of pollination by honeybees.

4. Science fiction has frequently explored the idea of time travel. For generations, people have been captivated by the notion of traveling either forward or backward in time, even though it is still only a theoretical notion.

What is the passage's primary subject?
a) The history of science fiction.
b) The feasibility of time travel.
c) The human fascination with time travel.
d) The technological advancements in time travel.

5. Ocean tides are triggered by the strong attraction of the moon and sun. Although the moon is more significant since it is nearer Earth, the tides are also greatly influenced by the mass of the sun.

In the text, what produces ocean tides?
a) The rotation of the Earth.
b) The gravitational pull of the moon and the sun.
c) The underwater topography.
d) The atmospheric pressure.

6. The post-impressionist painter Vincent van Gogh is renowned for his expressive and vibrant use of color. Despite his battles with mental illness, his distinctive style had a big influence on 20th-century art.

What is the passage mainly highlighting about Vincent van Gogh?
a) His battle with mental illness.

b) His influence on 20th-century art.
c) His financial success as an artist.
d) His early life and education.

7. The water cycle depends on the evaporation process. It involves the process of water changing from a liquid to a gas, mostly due to heat from the sun.

What is the passage's main point of emphasis?
a) The different states of water.
b) The role of the sun in the water cycle.
c) The importance of evaporation in the water cycle.
d) The impact of evaporation on climate change.

8. The dissemination of knowledge was completely transformed when Johannes Gutenberg invented the printing press in the fifteenth century. Large-scale production of books made them increasingly accessible for everyone.

What is the main point of the passage regarding the printing press?
a) The technical aspects of the printing press.
b) The biography of Johannes Gutenberg.
c) The impact of the printing press on knowledge dissemination.
d) The economic effects of the printing press.

9. Albert Einstein's theory of relativity offered new ideas about space and time as well as a new framework for all of science. The general theory of relativity and the special theory of relativity make up its two halves.

What is the passage's main topic?
a) The life achievements of Albert Einstein.
b) The components of the theory of relativity.
c) The impact of relativity on modern physics.
d) The difference between general and special relativity.

10. The Amazon rainforest, sometimes called the "lungs of the Earth," is essential to controlling the temperature of the planet. It makes oxygen and absorbs enormous volumes of carbon dioxide, which greatly improves the condition of the Earth as a whole.

What is the passage's main topic?
a) The biodiversity of the Amazon rainforest.
b) The deforestation issues in the Amazon.
c) The role of the Amazon in climate regulation.
d) The tourism potential of the Amazon rainforest.

11. The human brain is an extraordinarily intricate organ that performs a variety of cognitive tasks. It is separated into multiple areas, each of which has a distinct function, such as facilitating abstract thought or processing sensory data.

What is the passage's main topic?
a) The anatomy of the human brain.
b) The complexity and functions of the human brain.
c) The evolution of the human brain.
d) The medical conditions related to the brain.

12. The idea of popular rule is the foundation of the democratic concept, which dates back to ancient Greece. It focuses on protecting individual rights and involving citizens in political decision-making.

What is the passage primarily discussing?
a) The history of ancient Greece.
b) The principles of democracy.
c) The comparison of political systems.
d) The challenges faced by democracies.

13. One theory explaining the phenomenon known as temperature rise is a boom in greenhouse gases in the atmosphere of the globe. These gases trap heat, raising global temperatures gradually and causing substantial alterations to the environment.

What is the passage's main topic?
a) The causes of global warming.
b) The solutions to global warming.
c) The debate over global warming.
d) The effects of global warming on wildlife.

14. Art, literature, and science flourished throughout Europe's Renaissance, a time of cultural renewal. It marked the transition between the Middle Ages into the Modern Era.

What is the passage's main topic?
a) The art of the Renaissance period.
b) The scientific discoveries of the Renaissance.
c) The cultural significance of the Renaissance.
d) The political changes during the Renaissance.

15. A fundamental theory of physics known as quantum mechanics describes nature at the tiniest scales of atoms' and subatomic particles' energy levels. Its distinct concepts put classical physics to the test.

What is the passage's main topic?
a) The history of quantum mechanics.
b) The principles of quantum mechanics.
c) The applications of quantum mechanics.
d) The controversies surrounding quantum mechanics.

1. Answer: a) To describe the physical appearance of the Great Wall of China.
Explanation: The passage primarily focuses on describing the Great Wall's vastness and its path across various landscapes, rather than its history, construction, or preservation efforts.

2. Answer: b) To convert light energy into chemical energy.
Explanation: According to the passage, photosynthesis is a mechanism by the way plants switch light energy as chemical energy, which powers their operations.

3. Answer: c) The threats faced by honeybees.
Explanation: The passage discusses the crisis facing honeybees, specifically mentioning 'colony collapse disorder' and its various causes, indicating a focus on the threats to honeybees.

4. Answer: c) The human fascination with time travel.
Explanation: The passage talks about the concept of time travel being a subject of human fascination and its presence in science fiction, rather than its feasibility or history.

5. Answer: b) The gravitational pull of the moon and the sun.
Explanation: The text makes it rather evident that the forces of gravity of the sun and moon generates tides in the sea.

6. Answer: b) His influence on 20th-century art.
Explanation: The passage highlights Vincent van Gogh's impact on 20th-century art through his unique style, despite his personal struggles.

7. Answer: c) The importance of evaporation in the water cycle.
Explanation: The passage focuses on describing evaporation as a crucial part of the water cycle, emphasizing its role in transforming water from liquid to gas.

8. Answer: c) The impact of the printing press on knowledge dissemination.

Explanation: The text describes how Johannes Gutenberg's development of the printing press, which allowed books to be produced in large quantities, transformed the dissemination of knowledge.

9. Answer: b) The components of the theory of relativity.
Explanation: The passage describes the theory of relativity as consisting of two parts and its introduction of new concepts, focusing on the theory's components.

10. Answer: c) The role of the Amazon in climate regulation.
Explanation: The passage emphasizes the Amazon rainforest's critical role in regulating the global climate, particularly its function in absorbing carbon dioxide and producing oxygen.

11. Answer: b) The complexity and functions of the human brain.
Explanation: The passage discusses the human brain's complexity and its division into regions with specific cognitive functions.

12. Answer: b) The principles of democracy.
Explanation: The passage focuses on the foundational idea of democracy as rule by the people and emphasizes citizen participation and individual rights.

13. Answer: a) The causes of global warming.
Explanation: The passage focuses on the increase of greenhouse gases in the Earth's atmosphere as the cause of global warming.

14. Answer: c) The cultural significance of the Renaissance.
Explanation: The passage highlights the Renaissance as a period of cultural rebirth and its impact on art, literature, and science, marking a significant cultural shift.

15. Answer: b) The principles of quantum mechanics.
Explanation: The passage describes quantum mechanics as a fundamental theory in physics and mentions its unique principles, focusing on the theory's foundational aspects.

MATHEMATICS KNOWLEDGE

1. If $3x + 4 = 16$, what is the value of (x)?
   a) 4
   b) 5
   c) 6
   d) 7

2. Simplify the expression 5y - 3 + 2y + 6.
   a) 3y + 3
   b) 7y + 3
   c) 7y - 3
   d) 3y - 3

3. Which of the following is a polynomial expression?
   a) $1/x + 2$
   b) $x^2 - 4x + 7$
   c) $2^x + 3$
   d) x – square root of 2

4. Factor the expression $x^2 - 9$.
  a) $(x - 3)(x + 3)$
  b) $(x - 3)^2$
  c) $x(x - 9)$
  d) $(x + 3)^2$

5. What are the solutions to $x^2 - 5x + 6 = 0$?
  a) 2 and 3
  b) 1 and 6
  c) -2 and -3
  d) -1 and -6

6. Which of these equations is a quadratic?
  a) $x^2 + 4x - 5 = 0$
  b) $2x^3 - 3x + 1 = 0$
  c) $x - 5 = 0$
  d) $4x + 7 = 0$

7. What is the square root of 49?
  a) 7
  b) 14
  c) 21
  d) 28

8. What is the solution to the system of equations $2x + 3y = 10$ and $x - y = 2$?
  a) $x = 2, y = 0$
  b) $x = 4, y = 2$
  c) $x = 3, y = 1$
  d) $x = 1, y = 3$

9. Solve for (y) in the equation $3x - 2y = 6$ if $x = 4$.
  a) 3
  b) 0
  c) -3
  d) 6

10. For the quadratic equation $y = x^2 - 4x + 3$, what is the axis of symmetry?
  a) $x = 2$
  b) $x = -2$
  c) $y = 2$
  d) $y = -2$

11. What is the completed square form of $x^2 + 6x + 5$?
  a) $(x + 3)^2 - 4$
  b) $(x + 3)^2 + 4$
  c) $(x - 3)^2 - 4$
  d) $(x - 3)^2 + 4$

12. What is the discriminant of the quadratic equation $x^2 - 4x + 4 = 0$?
  a) 0
  b) 4
  c) 8

d) 16

13. In geometry, what is a line segment?
a) A part of a line with two endpoints
b) A part of a line with one endpoint
c) A straight path that extends infinitely in both directions
d) A curved line connecting two points

14. Which kind of angle is bigger than ninety degrees but smaller than one hundred eighty?
a) Acute angle
b) Right angle
c) Obtuse angle
d) Straight angle

15. Which of the following describes a polygon's properties?
a) Curved sides
b) Open figure
c) Closed figure with straight sides
d) Figure with only one side

16. What is the name for a right triangle's longest side?
a) Median
b) Altitude
c) Hypotenuse
d) Base

17. Which shape is a quadrilateral with two pairs of parallel sides?
a) Kite
b) Parallelogram
c) Trapezoid
d) Rhombus

18. What is an arc in a circle?
a) A straight line from the center to the circumference
b) The longest distance across the circle
c) A part of the circumference of a circle
d) The center point of the circle

19. What is the volume of a rectangular solid with length 5 cm, width 3 cm, and height 2 cm?
a) 30 cm³
b) 15 cm³
c) 10 cm³
d) 25 cm³

20. In the equation y = 2x + 3, what is the slope of this line?
a) 2
b) 3
c) -2
d) -3

1. Answer: a) 4
Explanation: Solving $3x + 4 = 16$ for (x) gives x = 4 as $3 \times 4 + 4 = 16$.

2. Answer: b) 7y + 3
Explanation: Simplifying 5y - 3 + 2y + 6 gives 7y + 3.

3. Answer: b) $x^2 - 4x + 7$
Explanation: A polynomial expression is a sum of terms with non-negative integer exponents. $x^2 - 4x + 7$ fits this definition.

4. Answer: a) (x - 3)(x + 3)
Explanation: Factoring $x^2 - 9$ gives (x - 3)(x + 3), as it is a difference of squares.

5. Answer: a) 2 and 3
Explanation: The solutions to $x^2 - 5x + 6 = 0$ are x = 2 and x = 3, as these values satisfy the equation.

6. Answer: a) $x^2 + 4x - 5 = 0$
Explanation: A quadratic equation is an equation of the second degree, typically in the form $ax^2 + bx + c = 0$.

7. Answer: a) 7
Explanation: The square root of 49 is 7, as 7 x 7 = 49.

8. Answer: c) x = 3, y = 1
Explanation: Solving the system of equations 2x + 3y = 10 and x - y = 2 gives x = 3 and y = 1.

9. Answer: c) -3
Explanation: Substituting x = 4 into 3x - 2y = 6 and solving for (y) gives y = -3.

10. Answer: a) x = 2
Explanation: The axis of symmetry for $y = x^2 - 4x + 3$ is x = 2, found by -b/(2a) in the quadratic formula.

11. Answer: a) $(x + 3)^2 - 4$
Explanation: Completing the square for $x^2 + 6x + 5$ gives $(x + 3)^2 - 4$.

12. Answer: a) 0
Explanation: The discriminant of $x^2 - 4x + 4 = 0$ is 0, indicating one real solution.

13. Answer: a) A part of a line with two endpoints
Explanation: Any portion of a line enclosed by two separate endpoints is referred to as a line segment.

14. Answer: c) Obtuse angle
Explanation: Over 90 degrees but under 180 degrees is an indication of an obtuse angle.

15. Answer: c) Closed figure with straight sides
Explanation: A closed figure composed of segments of straight lines constitutes a polygon.

16. Answer: c) Hypotenuse
Explanation: The hypotenuse is the longest side of a right triangle, opposite the right angle.

17. Answer: b) Parallelogram
Explanation: A quadrilateral having two pairs of parallel sides is identified as a parallelogram.

18. Answer: c) A part of the circumference of a circle
Explanation: An arc is a portion of the circumference of a circle.

19. Answer: a) 30 cm³

Explanation: The volume of a rectangular solid is found by multiplying length, width, and height: 5 x 3 x 2 = 30 cm³.

20. Answer: a) 2
Explanation: The slope of the line y = 2x + 3 is 2, as it is the coefficient of (x).

GENERAL SCIENCE

1. **Which of the following is a primary function of the human skeletal system?**
    a) Producing hormones
    b) Regulating body temperature
    c) Supporting body structure and facilitating movement
    d) Absorbing nutrients from food

2. **What is the primary function of the lungs in the human respiratory system?**
    a) To pump blood throughout the body
    b) To filter toxins from the blood
    c) To absorb nutrients from the air
    d) To facilitate the exchange of oxygen and carbon dioxide

3. **Which component of blood is primarily responsible for transporting oxygen to body tissues?**
    a) Plasma
    b) White blood cells
    c) Platelets
    d) Red blood cells

4. **What is the role of antigens in the human immune system?**
    a) They produce antibodies to fight infections.
    b) They are foreign substances that trigger an immune response.
    c) They heal damaged tissues.
    d) They regulate body temperature during an infection.

5. **In the human digestive system, which is the large intestine's main purpose?**
    a) Breaking down proteins
    b) Absorbing water and electrolytes from digested food
    c) Producing digestive enzymes
    d) Absorbing carbohydrates

6. **What is the main purpose of neurons in the neurological system of the human race?**
    a) To transport nutrients throughout the body
    b) To provide structural support to the brain and spinal cord
    c) To transmit information through electrical and chemical signals
    d) To filter blood in the brain

7. **What is the main purpose of meiosis in living organisms?**
    a) To produce identical cells for tissue repair
    b) To generate genetic diversity through sexual reproduction
    c) To convert energy into usable forms
    d) To create antibodies for the immune system

8. **Which of the following is an example of a human pathogen?**
    a) Red blood cell

b) Vitamin C
c) Escherichia coli
d) Oxygen molecule

9. What is the main function of mitosis in organisms with many cells?
a) To produce gametes for reproduction
b) To generate energy for cellular activities
c) To replicate cells for growth and repair
d) To absorb nutrients from food

10. What is the main outcome of cellular respiration in living organisms?
a) Production of oxygen
b) Release of carbon dioxide and water
c) Conversion of glucose into energy
d) Absorption of nutrients

11. What does the term "biosphere" refer to in ecology?
a) The layers of the Earth's atmosphere
b) The part of Earth where life exists, including land, water, and air
c) The deepest parts of the ocean
d) The upper layer of the Earth's crust

12. What role do scavengers play in an ecosystem?
a) They produce oxygen through photosynthesis.
b) They break down dead organisms and recycle nutrients.
c) They pollinate plants.
d) They regulate the population of other species.

13. What distinguishes eukaryotic cells from prokaryotic cells?
a) Eukaryotic cells lack a nucleus.
b) Eukaryotic cells have membrane-bound organelles.
c) Eukaryotic cells do not have DNA.
d) Eukaryotic cells are always unicellular.

14. How are sedimentary rocks typically formed?
a) By cooling and solidifying from magma
b) By high pressure and temperature deep within the Earth
c) By the accumulation and compaction of sediments
d) By meteorite impacts

15. What is the primary driver of the Earth's water cycle?
a) Plate tectonics
b) Solar energy
c) Gravity
d) Magnetic fields

16. In our solar system, which planet is nearest to the Sun?
a) Earth
b) Mars
c) Venus
d) Mercury

17. In physics, what does the term "mass" refer to?

a) The amount of space an object occupies
b) The weight of an object
c) The amount of matter in an object
d) The speed of an object

18. According to Newton's first law of motion, what will happen to an object in motion in the absence of external forces?
a) It will gradually slow down.
b) It will change direction.
c) It will continue moving at the same velocity.
d) It will accelerate.

19. What is an electric current?
a) The flow of heat through a conductor
b) The movement of magnetic fields
c) The flow of electric charge through a conductor
d) The storage of electric energy in a battery

20. What causes magnetism at the atomic level?
a) The motion of protons
b) The alignment of atomic nuclei
c) The movement of electrons
d) The vibration of atoms

1. Answer: c) Supporting body structure and facilitating movement
Explanation: The skeletal system supports the body structurally, permits mobility by acting as points of attachment for muscles, and safeguards important organs.

2. Answer: d) To facilitate the exchange of oxygen and carbon dioxide
Explanation: The primary function of the lungs is to exchange gases: they take in oxygen and expel carbon dioxide as a waste product of metabolism.

3. Answer: d) Red blood cells
Explanation: The job of red blood cells is to move carbon dioxide from the body's tissues back to the lungs and oxygen from the lungs to the body's tissues.

4. Answer: b) They are foreign substances that trigger an immune response.
Explanation: Antigens are substances that the immune system recognizes as foreign, triggering an immune response, often involving the production of antibodies.

5. Answer: b) Absorbing water and electrolytes from digested food
Explanation: The large intestine's major job is to transfer the body's worthless waste products and absorb water and electrolytes from the food that is still indigestible.

6. Answer: c) To transmit information through electrical and chemical signals
Explanation: Specialized cells called neurons use chemical and electrical impulses to transfer information throughout the body, allowing the brain to communicate with other body regions.

7. Answer: b) To generate genetic diversity through sexual reproduction
Explanation: Meiosis is a process that reduces the chromosome number by half and leads to the production of gametes (sperm and egg cells), introducing genetic diversity through sexual reproduction.

8. Answer: c) Escherichia coli

Explanation: Escherichia coli (E. coli) is a type of bacteria that can be a pathogen causing illness in humans, especially when it contaminates food or water.

9. Answer: c) To replicate cells for growth and repair
Explanation: In multicellular organisms, mitosis is a sort of cell division that produces two independent cells with the identical amount and type of chromosomes as the parent nucleus. This mechanism serves for development as well as repair.

10. Answer: c) Conversion of glucose into energy
Explanation: The process by which organisms transform biochemical energy from foods into adenosine triphosphate (ATP) and subsequently release waste products is known as cellular respiration.

11. Answer: b) The part of Earth where life exists, including land, water, and air
Explanation: The biosphere encompasses all ecosystems on Earth, including all living beings and their relationships, which includes their interactions with the elements of the lithosphere, hydrosphere, and atmosphere.

12. Answer: b) They break down dead organisms and recycle nutrients.
Explanation: By devouring dead plants and animals, scavengers contribute significantly to the ecosystem by dissolving them into simpler forms of matter and replenishing the environment with vital nutrients.

13. Answer: b) Eukaryotic cells have membrane-bound organelles.
Explanation: Eukaryotic cells are characterized by the presence of a nucleus enclosed within a membrane and the presence of membrane-bound organelles, distinguishing them from prokaryotic cells.

14. Answer: c) By the accumulation and compaction of sediments
Explanation: Sedimentary rocks are formed through the deposition and solidification of sediment, particularly on the floors of oceans and lakes.

15. Answer: b) Solar energy
Explanation: The Earth's water cycle is primarily driven by solar energy, which heats water in the oceans, causing it to evaporate and form clouds, leading to precipitation.

16. Answer: d) Mercury
Explanation: Mercury is the closest planet to the Sun in our solar system.

17. Answer: c) The amount of matter in an object
Explanation: A physical body's mass is a measurement of its opposition to movement in the presence of a net force. It also establishes how strongly it attracts other bodies with gravity.

18. Answer: c) It will continue moving at the same velocity.
Explanation: An object in motion will continue to move in the same direction and at the same speed unless an unbalanced external force acts upon it, according to Newton's first law of motion, sometimes referred to as the law of inertia.

19. Answer: c) The flow of electric charge through a conductor
Explanation: The flow of electrons in a wire or ions in another conductor that carries an electric charge is identified as an electric current.

20. Answer: c) The movement of electrons
Explanation: Magnetism at the atomic level is caused by the movement of electrons in atoms. Electrons have a property called spin, which contributes to their magnetic moment, leading to magnetism.

ELECTRONIC INFORMATION

1. Which substance is the most effective electrical conductor among all of them?
a) Rubber
b) Glass
c) Copper
d) Plastic

2. What is the voltage, or electrical potential difference, unit of measurement?
a) Ohm
b) Watt
c) Volt
d) Ampere

3. Which type of electrical circuit has multiple paths for current to flow?
a) Series Circuit
b) Parallel Circuit
c) Closed Circuit
d) Single Circuit

4. How is electrical power calculated in a circuit?
a) Voltage divided by resistance
b) Current plus resistance
c) Voltage times current
d) Resistance times current

5. What does an ampere measure?
a) Electrical resistance
b) Electrical power
c) Electrical current
d) Electrical voltage

6. What is a key characteristic of alternating current (AC)?
a) It flows in one direction only
b) It varies in magnitude and reverses direction periodically
c) It has a constant voltage
d) It cannot be transformed into higher or lower voltages

7. What does frequency in an AC circuit measure?
a) The number of electrons
b) The speed of current flow
c) The number of cycles per second
d) The resistance of the circuit

8. What is the purpose of grounding in electrical circuits?
a) To increase circuit speed
b) To reduce the risk of electric shock
c) To amplify the current
d) To store excess electricity

9. What is the primary function of a resistor in a circuit?
a) To store electrical energy

b) To increase voltage

c) To regulate or limit the flow of electrical current

d) To convert electrical energy into light

10. What is a rheostat primarily used for in a circuit?

a) To store charge

b) To convert AC to DC

c) To vary resistance

d) To increase voltage

11. What is the main purpose of a fuse in an electrical circuit?

a) To store electrical energy

b) To prevent overloading by breaking the circuit

c) To increase current flow

d) To convert energy types

12. What does capacitive reactance in an AC circuit resist?

a) Direct current

b) Changes in voltage

c) Constant voltage

d) Changes in current

13. Which material is typically used as a semiconductor?

a) Copper

b) Silicon

c) Gold

d) Iron

14. What is a transistor's main use in an electronic circuit?

a) To store electrical charge

b) To act as a switch or signal amplifier

c) To convert AC to DC

d) To increase resistance

15. Which of the following is a property of all magnets?

a) They generate electricity when heated

b) They have at least one north and one south pole

c) They are always made of iron

d) They can store electrical charge

1. Answer: c) Copper

Explanation: Because of its exceptional electrical conductivity, copper is a great material for electrical components and wiring. Unlike rubber and plastic, which are insulators, copper allows for efficient flow of electric current.

2. Answer: c) Volt

Explanation: The unit of measurement for voltage, or electrical potential difference, is volts. It stands for the force that propels current across an electrical circuit.

3. Answer: b) Parallel Circuit

Explanation: In a parallel circuit, there are multiple paths for current to flow, unlike a series circuit where there is only one path.

4. Answer: c) Voltage times current

Explanation: Electrical power is calculated by multiplying voltage (potential difference) by current (flow of charge). This formula is represented as P = VI, where P is power, V is voltage, and I is current.

5. Answer: c) Electrical current
Explanation: Electrical current, or the movement of electric charge, can be expressed in amps, or amperes.

6. Answer: b) It varies in magnitude and reverses direction periodically
Explanation: Different from direct current (DC), which operates solely in one way, alternating current (AC) is defined by its periodic shift in direction and variation in magnitude.

7. Answer: c) The number of cycles per second
Explanation: The frequency of an AC circuit indicates how many times the current reverses course in a second. It is measured in hertz (Hz).

8. Answer: b) To reduce the risk of electric shock
Explanation: By creating a secure route for extra electricity to reach the earth, grounding lowers the possibility of electrical fires and electric shock.

9. Answer: c) To regulate or limit the flow of electrical current
Explanation: Resistors are used in circuits to control the amount of current by providing resistance, which limits the flow of electric charge.

10. Answer: c) To vary resistance
Explanation: Rheostats are movable resistors which alter the resistance in an electrical system to control current.

11. Answer: b) To prevent overloading by breaking the circuit
Explanation: Fuses melt and break circuits when the current beyond a safe threshold, shielding circuits from excessive current.

12. Answer: b) Changes in voltage
Explanation: Capacitive reactance in an AC circuit resists changes in voltage. It is the opposition that a capacitor offers to changes in voltage due to its capacity to store and release energy.

13. Answer: b) Silicon
Explanation: Silicon is a widely used semiconductor material in electronic devices due to its ability to conduct electricity under certain conditions, making it essential for transistors and integrated circuits.

14. Answer: b) To act as a switch or signal amplifier
Explanation: Transistors are essential components of both digital and analog circuits because they can switch or amplify electrical impulses in electronic circuits.

15. Answer: b) They have at least one north and one south pole
Explanation: Every magnet has a minimum of one north and one south pole. The essential characteristic of magnets is the attraction between opposite poles and the repulsion between like poles.

AUTO AND SHOP INFORMATION

1. In an internal combustion engine, what is the primary function of the crankshaft?
   a) To control the opening and closing of engine valves
   b) To convert the reciprocating motion of pistons into rotary motion

c) To pump coolant through the engine

d) To ignite the fuel-air mixture

2. During the intake stroke of a four-stroke engine, what occurs?

    a) The piston compresses the air-fuel mixture

    b) The spark plug ignites the air-fuel mixture

    c) The piston moves down, drawing in a mixture of air and fuel

    d) Exhaust gases are expelled from the cylinder

3. Which of the following is NOT a common cylinder configuration in an internal combustion engine?

    a) V6

    b) Inline-4

    c) Radial-8

    d) Flat-6

4. In an internal combustion engine, combustion occurs when:

    a) The piston reaches its lowest point

    b) The air-fuel mixture is compressed and ignited by the spark plug

    c) The exhaust valve opens

    d) The intake valve closes

5. Which component is NOT part of a car's cooling system?

    a) Radiator

    b) Thermostat

    c) Fuel injector

    d) Water pump

6. What is the primary purpose of the lubrication system in a car engine?

    a) To cool the engine

    b) To reduce friction between moving parts

    c) To clean the engine

    d) To increase fuel efficiency

7. Which type of fuel system uses electronic sensors to regulate fuel injection?

    a) Carburetor

    b) Mechanical fuel injection

    c) Electronic fuel injection

    d) Gravity feed system

8. What is the role of the Powertrain Control Module (PCM) in a vehicle?

    a) To control the vehicle's audio system

    b) To regulate the air conditioning system

    c) To manage the engine and transmission performance

    d) To control the vehicle's lighting system

9. In an ignition system, what is the role of the primary coil winding?

    a) To ignite the fuel-air mixture

    b) To convert high voltage to low voltage

    c) To create a magnetic field that induces high voltage in the secondary coil

    d) To store electrical energy for the spark plugs

10. What is the primary function of spark plugs in an internal combustion engine?

    a) To compress the air-fuel mixture

b) To ignite the air-fuel mixture

c) To regulate the flow of fuel

d) To filter engine oil

11. How does a Distributorless Ignition System (DIS) differ from a traditional ignition system?

a) It uses a distributor to direct high voltage

b) It directly controls the timing and firing of the spark plugs

c) It relies on mechanical timing

d) It uses a single coil for all cylinders

12. What is the primary function of a catalytic converter in a vehicle?

a) To reduce engine noise

b) To increase fuel efficiency

c) To convert harmful emissions into less harmful gases

d) To cool the exhaust gases

13. What is the primary purpose of a car's alternator?

a) To start the engine

b) To charge the battery and power the electrical system while the engine runs

c) To control the ignition timing

d) To regulate fuel injection

14. What is the main function of a vehicle's drivetrain system?

a) To control the steering of the vehicle

b) To transmit power from the engine to the drive wheels

c) To absorb shocks from road surfaces

d) To cool the engine

15. What distinguishes an All-Wheel Drive (AWD) system from other drivetrain systems?

a) It only powers the front wheels

b) It provides power to all four wheels continuously

c) It is only active when the vehicle is off-road

d) It powers the rear wheels only

16. In automotive terms, what is a transaxle designed to do?

a) To absorb shocks from uneven road surfaces

b) To combine the functions of a transmission and axle in one unit

c) To distribute air to the engine

d) To control the vehicle's braking system

17. What is the primary role of shock absorbers in a vehicle?

a) To maintain tire contact with the road

b) To cool the engine

c) To reduce the vehicle's speed

d) To filter engine oil

18. What is the purpose of the brake fluid reservoir in a vehicle?

a) To store fuel for the engine

b) To hold brake fluid used in the braking system

c) To collect exhaust gases

d) To lubricate the engine

19. What is a micrometer primarily used for in a workshop?

a) To measure electrical current
b) To check fluid levels
c) To measure small distances with precision
d) To tighten bolts and nuts

20. What is a ball-peen hammer typically used for in a workshop?
a) To check tire pressure
b) For shaping metal and closing rivets
c) To cut through metal
d) To measure angles

21. What is the primary use of punches in a workshop?
a) To inflate tires
b) To drive or mark material when struck with a hammer
c) To measure distances
d) To hold objects in place

22. What is the main function of wrenches in mechanical work?
a) To cut through materials
b) To measure angles
c) To provide grip and apply torque to turn objects
d) To absorb shocks

23. What does oxyacetylene welding primarily involve?
a) Using a high-frequency electric current
b) Melting base metal using a flame from gas
c) Cooling metal components
d) Applying a protective coating to metal surfaces

24. What is the primary purpose of clamps in a workshop?
a) To measure distances
b) To secure objects tightly together
c) To cut materials
d) To inflate tires

25. In woodworking, what is the main use of a plane?
a) To measure wood thickness
b) To bend wood
c) To flatten or shape wood
d) To join wood pieces together

1. Answer: b) To convert the reciprocating motion of pistons into rotary motion
Explanation: An internal combustion engine's crankshaft is made to transform the pistons' up-and-down (reciprocating) motion into a rotating (rotary) motion, which powers the wheels of the car.

2. Answer: c) The piston moves down, drawing in a mixture of air and fuel
Explanation: A four-stroke engine's intake stroke occurs as the piston descends, creating a vacuum that allows fuel and air to enter the cylinder through the open intake valve.

3. Answer: c) Radial-8
Explanation: Radial-8 is not a common configuration for automotive internal combustion engines. Common configurations include V6, Inline-4, and Flat-6.

4. Answer: b) The air-fuel mixture is compressed and ignited by the spark plug

Explanation: In an internal combustion engine, combustion occurs when the compressed air-fuel mixture in the cylinder is ignited by the spark plug, causing an explosion that drives the piston.

5. Answer: c) Fuel injector

Explanation: The fuel injector is part of the fuel system, not the cooling system. Components of the cooling system include the radiator, thermostat, and water pump.

6. Answer: b) To reduce friction between moving parts

Explanation: The primary purpose of the lubrication system in a car engine is to provide oil to the engine's moving parts, reducing friction, heat, and wear.

7. Answer: c) Electronic fuel injection

Explanation: Electronic fuel injection systems use electronic sensors and a computer to regulate fuel injection, providing precise control over the air-fuel mixture.

8. Answer: c) To manage the engine and transmission performance

Explanation: The Powertrain Control Module (PCM) is responsible for managing and coordinating the performance of the engine and transmission, optimizing efficiency and power output.

9. Answer: c) To create a magnetic field that induces high voltage in the secondary coil

Explanation: The primary coil winding in an ignition system creates a magnetic field when energized. The secondary coil winding experiences a high voltage due to this field, and the spark plugs use this voltage to produce a spark.

10. Answer: b) To ignite the air-fuel mixture

Explanation: The primary function of spark plugs in an internal combustion engine is to ignite the compressed air-fuel mixture in the cylinders, initiating the combustion process.

11. Answer: b) It directly controls the timing and firing of the spark plugs

Explanation: A Distributorless Ignition System (DIS) eliminates the need for a distributor by using sensors and electronic control to directly manage the timing and firing of the spark plugs.

12. Answer: c) To convert harmful emissions into less harmful gases

Explanation: By changing toxic chemicals such as nitrogen oxides and carbon monoxide into less harmful ones, the catalytic converter in an automobile's exhaust system lowers harmful emissions.

13. Answer: b) To charge the battery and power the electrical system while the engine runs

Explanation: The alternator in a car's electrical system generates electrical power to charge the battery and run the electrical components of the vehicle while the engine is operating.

14. Answer: b) To transmit power from the engine to the drive wheels

Explanation: The power produced by the engine of a car is transferred to the drive wheels by the drivetrain system, allowing the car to move.

15. Answer: b) It provides power to all four wheels continuously

Explanation: An All-Wheel Drive (AWD) system continuously provides power to all four wheels of the vehicle, enhancing traction and handling under various driving conditions.

16. Answer: b) To combine the functions of a transmission and axle in one unit

Explanation: A transaxle is a single mechanical unit that combines the functions of a transmission (gear shifting) and an axle (power delivery to the wheels), commonly used in front-wheel-drive vehicles.

17. Answer: a) To maintain tire contact with the road

Explanation: Shock absorbers in a vehicle help to absorb and dampen the impact from road surfaces, maintaining tire contact with the road and providing a smoother ride.

18. Answer: b) To hold brake fluid used in the braking system
Explanation: The hydraulic oil that enables a brake system to transmit force from the pedal to the brake assemblies at the wheels is kept in reserve in a vehicle's brake fluid reservoir.

19. Answer: c) To measure small distances with precision
Explanation: A micrometer is a high-precision measuring instrument used in workshops to measure thin materials, including bolt diameters or metal sheet thicknesses, with extreme accuracy.

20. Answer: b) For shaping metal and closing rivets
Explanation: A ball-peen hammer, with its flat striking face and rounded peen, is commonly used in metalworking for shaping metal and closing rivets.

21. Answer: b) To drive or mark material when struck with a hammer
Explanation: Punches are tools used in conjunction with a hammer to drive or mark materials, such as driving out pins or making indentations for drilling.

22. Answer: c) To provide grip and apply torque to turn objects
Explanation: In mechanical work, wrenches are instruments that offer mechanical advantage and grip when applying torque to turn things such as nuts and bolts.

23. Answer: b) Melting base metal using a flame from gas
Explanation: Oxyacetylene welding involves using a flame produced by a mixture of acetylene and oxygen gases to melt the base metal and create a weld.

24. Answer: b) To secure objects tightly together
Explanation: In workshops, clamps are used to hold or secure objects firmly together, preventing separation or movement while doing operations like sawing or gluing.

25. Answer: c) To flatten or shape wood
Explanation: In woodworking, planes are used to flatten, smooth, or shape wood surfaces by shaving off thin layers of wood as the tool is pushed along the surface.

MECHANICAL COMPREHENSION

1. In a hydraulic press, if a force of 200N is applied to compress a material, and the area of contact is 0.5 square meters, what is the compression pressure exerted on the material?
   a) 100 Pascals
   b) 400 Pascals
   c) 200 Pascals
   d) 300 Pascals

2. If a car of mass 1500 kg accelerates at 2 m/s², what is the force exerted by the engine?
   a) 3000 N
   b) 750 N
   c) 1500 N
   d) 2500 N

3. The air pressure is approximately 101,325 Pascals at sea level. If a weather balloon ascends to a height where the pressure is half the sea level pressure, what would be the new pressure reading?
   a) 50,662.5 Pascals
   b) 202,650 Pascals
   c) 75,000 Pascals
   d) 25,000 Pascals

4. A tank is being filled with water at a rate of 3 liters per minute. After 30 minutes, how much water would be left in the tank?
   a) 90 liters
   b) 60 liters
   c) 120 liters
   d) 150 liters

5. If a wrench is 0.5 meters long and a force of 20 N is applied perpendicularly at its end, what is the torque produced?
   a) 40 Nm
   b) 10 Nm
   c) 20 Nm
   d) 30 Nm

6. A worker pushes a box with a force of 50 N for a distance of 3 meters. To what extent is the box completed?
   a) 150 Joules
   b) 100 Joules
   c) 200 Joules
   d) 50 Joules

7. When a 2 kilogram object moves at a speed of 3 m/s, how much kinetic energy is it carrying?
   a) 9 Joules
   b) 18 Joules
   c) 6 Joules
   d) 12 Joules

8. Five meters above the floor, a 10-kg object is grasped. What is the energy potential of it?
   a) 500 Joules
   b) 50 Joules
   c) 100 Joules
   d) 250 Joules

9. If a machine does 200 Joules of work in 10 seconds, what is its power output?
   a) 20 Watts
   b) 10 Watts
   c) 30 Watts
   d) 40 Watts

10. A lever has two meters for the load arm and four meters for the effort arm. What is its mechanical advantage?
    a) 2
    b) 1
    c) 4
    d) 0.5

11. In a pulley system with 3 supporting ropes lifting a load, what is the mechanical advantage of the system?

a) 3
b) 2
c) 4
d) 1

12. If a compound machine consists of three simple machines with mechanical advantages of 2, 4, and 3 respectively, what is the total mechanical advantage of the compound machine?
a) 24
b) 9
c) 12
d) 6

13. Which of the following materials is known for its high malleability?
a) Glass
b) Steel
c) Gold
d) Diamond

14. When a ball is thrown upwards, which principle explains why it eventually stops ascending and starts descending?
a) Newton's First Law
b) Gravity
c) Air resistance
d) Friction

15. In a bridge supported by three equally spaced pillars, where would the maximum stress likely be observed?
a) In the middle pillar
b) In the end pillars
c) Equally in all pillars
d) At the ends of the bridge, away from the pillars

1. Answer: b) 400 Pascals
Explanation: Compression pressure is calculated as force divided by area. Here, 200N / 0.5m² = 400N/m² or 400 Pascals.

2. Answer: a) 3000 N
Explanation: Newton's second law states that force equals mass times acceleration. Here, 1500 kg × 2 m/s² = 3000 N.

3. Answer: a) 50,662.5 Pascals
Explanation: Half of the sea level pressure (101,325 Pascals) is 50,662.5 Pascals.

4. Answer: a) 90 liters
Explanation: The tank fills at 3 liters per minute. Over 30 minutes, it fills 3 liters/minute × 30 minutes = 90 liters.

5. Answer: b) 10 Nm
Explanation: Torque is calculated as force times distance. Here, 20 N × 0.5 m = 10 Nm.

6. Answer: a) 150 Joules
Explanation: Work is force times distance. Here, 50 N × 3 m = 150 Joules.

7. Answer: b) 18 Joules
Explanation: Kinetic energy is 1/2 mass times velocity squared. Here, 1/2 × 2 kg × (3 m/s)² = 18 Joules.

8. Answer: a) 500 Joules

Explanation: Potential energy is mass times gravity times height. Here, 10 kg × 9.8 m/s² (gravity) × 5 m = 490 Joules, approximately 500 Joules.

9. Answer: a) 20 Watts
Explanation: Power is work divided by time. Here, 200 Joules / 10 seconds = 20 Watts.

10. Answer: a) 2
Explanation: Mechanical advantage is effort distance divided by load distance. Here, 4 m / 2 m = 2.

11. Answer: a) 3
Explanation: For a given number of supporting ropes, the pulley system's mechanical advantage is equal. Here, it's 3.

12. Answer: c) 12
Explanation: The sum of the individual advantages yields the overall mechanical advantage. Here, 2 × 4 × 3 = 24.

13. Answer: c) Gold
Explanation: Gold is known for its high malleability, allowing it to be shaped and formed easily.

14. Answer: b) Gravity
Explanation: Gravity is the force that pulls the ball back to the ground after it stops ascending.

15. Answer: a) In the middle pillar
Explanation: The maximum stress in a bridge supported by equally spaced pillars is typically observed in the middle pillar due to the distribution of weight and tension.

CHAPTER 7 – CONCLUSIONS

As we come to an end of this extensive ASVAB Study Guide, it's important to take stock of your trip thus far. This guide was carefully designed to provide you the skills and information you need to not only take the ASVAB, but also do well on your first try. Your success was the focus of each and every chapter, hint, and practice question that was created.

The ASVAB requires a special combination of intelligence and effort, making it a stepping stone to your military career. This guide was meant to give you both. With the help of thorough subject reviews, challenging practice exams, and cutting-edge study methods, you've been given the resources you need to realize your dream. Keep in mind that the caliber of your performance will frequently correspond with the caliber of your preparation.

It's critical to recognize that success is a path of learning and growth rather than only passing an exam. You've grown more knowledgeable, more disciplined, and better at solving problems. These are priceless abilities that go beyond the ASVAB; they will benefit you in many areas of your life.

It's crucial to understand, though, that occasionally, despite our greatest efforts, results can not live up to our expectations. Don't allow disappointment cloud your judgment if the results of the ASVAB don't go in your favor. Failure is a chance for personal development rather than a reflection on your ability. It's an opportunity to reevaluate, reconnect, and improve your strategy.

Recall that conquering obstacles is a must for any significant accomplishment. If you encounter adversity, use it to strengthen your resolve rather than to lower your spirits. Generally, the key to success is perseverance. The road to achieving your dreams will almost certainly be paved with roadblocks and diversions. But your unwavering commitment to your goals is what will get you there.

This guide was as more than simply an exam pass aid; it was a traveling companion that helped you accomplish a big life goal. Take the knowledge, abilities, and confidence you've gained with you as you conclude this chapter and move forward to the future. Recall that the ASVAB is a demonstration of your commitment and drive for success as much as a test of your knowledge.

As you proceed, acknowledge your accomplishments and have confidence in your future potential. Your desire to join the military is not just a job; it's a pledge to serve and a demonstration of your inner fortitude. Use this guide as a reminder of what you can do if you put in the necessary effort, are persistent, and have faith in yourself.

To sum up, we hope that this ASVAB Study Guide will serve as a stepping stone for you to success. Remember that you are flipping the pages of your trip towards a promising and bright future as you turn each page. Maintain your motivation, stand up, and advance with assurance. Dreams can come true; every step you take will take you one step closer to your destination.

Made in the USA
Monee, IL
11 April 2024

56776455R00063